CGP

GCSE AQA English Language
Spoken Language
Study and Practice Book

This book is for anyone doing
GCSE AQA English Language at higher level.

It's a **step-by-step guide** to becoming an expert on the Unit 3 Part C
Spoken Language Study controlled assessment.

It's got **everything you need** — study notes, worked examples, practice questions,
practice examples and an assessment-focused guide to analysing
spoken language — to help you get **the grade you want**.

It's ideal for use as a classroom study book
or a revision guide.

What CGP is all about

Our sole aim here at CGP is to produce the highest quality
books — carefully written, immaculately presented and
dangerously close to being funny.

Then we work our socks off to get them out to you
— at the cheapest possible prices.

CONTENTS

Section Four — Multi-Modal Talk

Section Five — The Controlled Assessment

Published by CGP

Editors:
Claire Boulter
Polly Cotterill
Edmund Robinson

Produced with:
Alison Smith
Nicola Woodfin

Contributors:
Tony Flanagan
Jan Greenway

With thanks to Edward Robinson and Elisabeth Sanderson for the proofreading.

ISBN: 978 1 84762 546 5

Groovy website: www.cgpbooks.co.uk
Jolly bits of clipart from CorelDRAW®
Printed by Elanders Ltd, Newcastle upon Tyne.

Based on the classic CGP style created by Richard Parsons.

Photocopying — it's dull, grey and sometimes a bit naughty. Luckily, it's dead cheap, easy and quick to order
more copies of this book from CGP — just call us on 0870 750 1242. Phew!

How to Use This Book

This book will help you with the <u>spoken language</u> controlled assessment for <u>Unit 3 Part C</u> of the <u>AQA</u> <u>English Language GCSE</u>. It's worth <u>10%</u> of your <u>overall mark</u>, so you'd be a fool not to get it in the bag.

The Assessment Objectives tell you what Skills you need

The <u>assessment objectives</u> are the things the <u>exam board</u> says you need to be able to do for this bit of the GCSE. Don't worry — there aren't very many of them. Put simply, you have to:

1) Understand <u>how</u> and <u>why</u> spoken language is <u>different</u> in different <u>contexts</u>.

2) Evaluate how <u>real-life speech</u> varies between different <u>people</u>, <u>social groups</u> and <u>regions</u>.

3) Understand people's <u>attitudes</u> to different forms of English (e.g. <u>standard</u> and <u>non-standard</u>, different <u>dialects</u>, <u>slang</u> etc.).

Each Section looks at a Different Aspect of Spoken Language

1 <u>Section One</u> gives you a brief intro on how to study <u>spoken language</u> and the kind of things you need to look out for.

2 <u>Section Two</u> looks at different <u>dialects</u> (<u>regional</u>, <u>social</u> and <u>individual</u>) and how people <u>react differently</u> to different <u>forms</u> of spoken language.

Alfonso couldn't work out whether the bull was reacting to his spoken language or his dress sense.

3 <u>Section Three</u> gets into different <u>genres</u> (types) of spoken language — e.g. <u>public talk</u>, <u>TV</u> and <u>radio</u>.

4 <u>Section Four</u> is about <u>multi-modal talk</u> — <u>written language</u> that contains elements of <u>spoken language</u>. It includes things like <u>texting</u>, <u>instant messaging</u> and <u>emails</u>.

<u>Sections Two to Four</u> contain the following stuff to turn you into a spoken language <u>expert</u>:

- Some <u>information</u> about the topic.
- <u>Worked examples</u> of some <u>data</u>, showing you the factual stuff in action.
- Some <u>practice questions</u> so you can check that you've understood the topic.
- <u>Practice examples</u> to give you a chance to <u>try out</u> what you've learnt.

5 Finally, <u>Section Five</u> is your all-singing, all-dancing guide to the <u>controlled assessment</u>, with loads of <u>advice</u> about how to <u>gather data</u>, as well as some <u>sample tasks</u> and <u>answers</u>.

It's English, Jim, but not as we know it...

So, your work for this unit is almost certain to include watching TV, texting your mates or playing around in chat rooms. Put like that, it doesn't sound too scary, does it...

Introduction to Spoken Language

You use <u>spoken language</u> every time you want to <u>communicate</u> with someone else — whether it's to order a milkshake, make a speech in your school assembly or chat to your best mate.

Spoken Language comes in many Forms

1) <u>Spoken conversations</u> are different from written language because they tend to be <u>spontaneous</u> and <u>unpredictable</u>.

2) Speech contains tiny, subtle clues about the <u>speaker</u> and the <u>context</u> of the speech. By listening to <u>what</u> people say, and <u>how</u> they say it, you can work out loads of stuff about <u>who</u> they are, <u>where</u> they're from and <u>what</u> they're doing. Pretty cool, eh?

3) Strange as it may sound, it's much <u>easier</u> to study <u>spoken language</u> if you can get it down in <u>writing</u>. There are lots of different <u>written forms</u> that spoken language can take. For example:

> • <u>Transcript</u> — this is when <u>speech</u> (e.g. a conversation between two people) is written down.
>
> • <u>Script</u> — this is when language is <u>written</u> down in order to be <u>spoken</u>, e.g. a TV script.
>
> • <u>Multi-modal talk</u> — this includes things like <u>emails</u>, <u>instant messaging</u> and <u>text messaging</u>. Although it's written, it also contains lots of <u>spoken language features</u>.

You'll be analysing data in one of these forms.

Listen out for Sounds, Vocabulary and Grammar

There are <u>three</u> main things to listen out for when you <u>analyse spoken language</u>.

1) <u>How the language sounds</u>
  • The speaker's <u>pronunciation</u> might tell you something about <u>where</u> they're from — their <u>regional background</u>.
  • It might also tell you about their <u>social background</u> — e.g. that they're middle class.

2) <u>The speaker's vocabulary</u>
  • Some words are only used in certain <u>regional dialects</u> (e.g. 'bezz' is used in Yorkshire and Lincolnshire to describe going somewhere quickly).
  • People's vocabulary <u>changes</u> according to <u>who</u> they're talking to, e.g. you probably use more <u>slang</u> when you talk to your mates than when you talk to a teacher.

3) <u>The speaker's grammar</u>
  • <u>Non-standard grammar</u> gives you clues about <u>where</u> the speaker's <u>from</u>.
  • For instance, lots of dialects in the <u>north</u> of England use 'he were' rather than 'he was'.

• You can also work out things like the <u>context</u> of a conversation.

• For example, when you're paying for something in a shop you'll probably use <u>set phrases</u> like '<u>there you go</u>' and '<u>thanks</u>'.

• These routines are different types of <u>discourse</u>. They <u>change</u> depending on the <u>context</u> you're in (see p.15).

Eee, that were reet interesting...

Who knew you could tell so much about a person just by looking at how they talk. It makes me a bit paranoid, actually. That's why I've adopted a fake Yorkshire accent, just in case they're watching me...

Speech Features

I know it all sounds a bit scary, but we'll take it slowly. The next couple of pages give you a brief intro to some of the things you need to look out for when you're analysing a conversation.

People Usually try to be Polite to each other

There are different ways of making sure that you don't fall out with the people you're talking to:

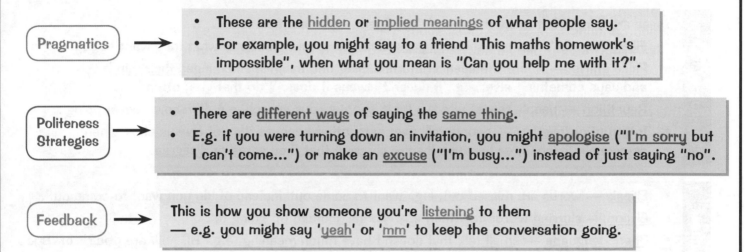

Pragmatics →
- These are the hidden or implied meanings of what people say.
- For example, you might say to a friend "This maths homework's impossible", when what you mean is "Can you help me with it?".

Politeness Strategies →
- There are different ways of saying the same thing.
- E.g. if you were turning down an invitation, you might apologise ("I'm sorry but I can't come...") or make an excuse ("I'm busy...") instead of just saying "no".

Feedback →
This is how you show someone you're listening to them
— e.g. you might say 'yeah' or 'mm' to keep the conversation going.

Language Changes depending on Who you're talking to

1) You can tell a lot about the relationship between people by how they talk to one another. People are usually more formal and polite with strangers or their superiors than with friends and family.

> E.g. if someone says "Open that door", they're probably talking to a friend, a family member or someone they have authority over, but if they say "I'm sorry, but would you mind opening the door?" they're probably talking to a superior or someone they don't know very well.

2) Address terms (what people call each other) can reveal a lot about their relationship. For example, you'd probably call your headmaster 'sir' rather than 'mate'.

3) It's often useful to think about who's got more power in a conversation and how they show this.

Spoken Language has Paralinguistic Features

'Paralinguistic features' just means the aspects of speech that aren't words — e.g. hand gestures and tone of voice. They can change the meaning of what you're saying:

- Stress — emphasising particular words can change the meaning of the sentence (e.g. 'He'll be here tomorrow' has a different meaning from 'He'll be here tomorrow').
- Tone — how something is said (e.g. someone's tone could be playful or sarcastic).
- Volume — e.g. loudness might show anger, excitement or confidence.

"Billy, why do you keep sighing and rolling your eyes?"

"I'm practising my paralinguistic features, Miss." There's a lot to take in, so make sure it all makes sense by listening to conversations and trying to pick out some of the things on this page.

Speech Features

Safety goggles on, it's <u>transcript</u> time. These are absolute <u>gold</u> when you're <u>analysing spoken language</u>.

Transcripts help you Analyse Spoken Language

1) Recordings of speech can be <u>transcribed</u> (written down) to make them <u>easier to study</u>.

2) <u>Speech</u> contains some weird <u>features</u> — here are some you could listen out for:

Non-fluency features

These are things that make the speech <u>less fluent</u> — for example...

- <u>Fillers</u> (e.g. 'er', 'um') — these <u>fill gaps</u> while the speaker thinks of what they want to say.
- <u>False starts</u> — where the speaker starts saying one thing, then <u>changes their mind</u> and says something else, e.g. 'it doesn't always it doesn't do that very often'.
- <u>Repetition</u> — people repeat words a lot in spontaneous speech, e.g. 'I'm never never going'.
- <u>Interruption/overlap</u> — people <u>talk over</u> each other because it's not always clear when someone's finished, or because they're showing that they <u>agree</u> or <u>disagree</u>.

Other features

- <u>Ellipsis</u> — words are missed out, e.g. 'want to come out' instead of '<u>do you</u> want to come out'.
- <u>Elision</u> — <u>slurring</u> words together, e.g. 'gonna' instead of 'going to'.
- <u>Phatic language</u> — <u>small talk</u> that doesn't have much <u>meaning</u>, e.g. 'Hi, how are you?', or 'Bye'.
- <u>Deixis</u> — language that can only be understood in the <u>context</u> of the <u>conversation</u>, e.g. pointing to an item on a menu and saying 'I'll have that'.
- '<u>Vague</u>' language — e.g. saying 'sort of', 'like' or 'lots'.

> If you feel happy using these terms then go for it, but don't worry too much if you can't.

This is how the Transcripts look in This Book

- We've written down <u>everything</u> the speakers say, including '<u>filler</u>' words like 'er' and 'um'.
- We <u>haven't</u> used <u>commas</u>, <u>full stops</u>, <u>question marks</u> etc. Instead, <u>pauses</u> are shown like this:

  (.) = <u>micropause</u> (less than 1 second)   (2) = a <u>pause</u> showing the number of seconds it lasts.

- <u>Interruptions</u> or <u>overlap</u> are shown using the symbol // at the point where someone's interrupted.

So... here's what a <u>transcript</u> of a <u>conversation</u> between <u>two people</u> might look like:

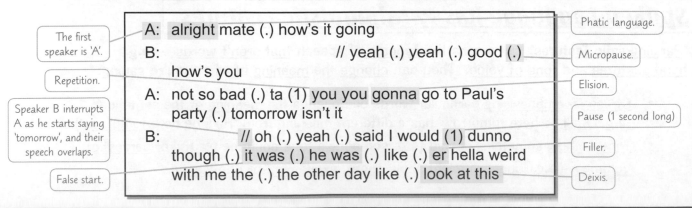

The first speaker is 'A'.

Repetition.

Speaker B interrupts A as he starts saying 'tomorrow', and their speech overlaps.

False start.

A: alright mate (.) how's it going

B: // yeah (.) yeah (.) good (.) how's you

A: not so bad (.) ta (1) you you gonna go to Paul's party (.) tomorrow isn't it

B: // oh (.) yeah (.) said I would (1) dunno though (.) it was (.) he was (.) like (.) er hella weird with me the (.) the other day like (.) look at this

Phatic language.

Micropause.

Elision.

Pause (1 second long)

Filler.

Deixis.

I was transcribed once — it didn't half sting...

Don't worry if all this seems a bit daunting at first — by the end of the book it'll be second nature and you'll be pointing out elision and phatic language like a spoken language pro...

Accent and Dialect

Regional <u>accents</u> and <u>dialects</u> can be a bit confusing if you're not from that area of the country. It's <u>not</u> always just the <u>pronunciation</u> that changes — the <u>actual words</u> people use can change too.

Your Accent is How you Pronounce words

1) People with different <u>accents</u> <u>pronounce</u> the same words in <u>different ways</u>.

2) An accent can be <u>part</u> of a dialect. But it's <u>different</u> from dialect because it just refers to <u>how</u> you say words, not the words themselves.

Accents depend on Where the Speaker's From...

1) <u>Regional accents</u> are <u>different</u> depending on which part of the country the speaker's from.

2) In <u>England</u>, most people can tell the big difference between <u>northern accents</u> and <u>southern accents</u>. The main differences between them are the <u>vowel sounds</u>. For example:

- Someone with a <u>northern accent</u> would say '<u>grass</u>' with a <u>short vowel sound</u>, to sound like '<u>cat</u>'.
- Someone with a <u>southern accent</u> would say '<u>grass</u>' with a <u>long vowel sound</u>, like '<u>grarss</u>'.

...and on their Social Background

1) A <u>social accent</u> is the result of someone's <u>class</u> or <u>background</u>, rather than where they're from.

2) The most <u>familiar</u> English social accent is <u>Received Pronunciation</u> (see p.10).

3) When someone speaks with this accent, you often <u>can't tell</u> which part of the country they're from.

Your Dialect is the Words you use

1) A <u>dialect</u> is a <u>variety</u> of a language. The term <u>dialect</u> is usually used to describe language that's specific to a <u>certain place</u>, e.g. 'Cornish dialect' is the dialect people use in Cornwall.

2) Dialects have specific features of <u>vocabulary</u>, <u>grammar</u> and <u>pronunciation</u>. For example:

Vocab	Different dialects have different words for things, e.g. in Northern Ireland and Scotland, people say '<u>wee</u>' to mean '<u>little</u>'.
Grammar	Regional dialects contain <u>non-standard</u> grammar, e.g. missing plurals — "it costs four <u>pound</u>" (instead of 'pounds').
Pronunciation	Most regional dialects have an <u>accent</u> to go with them. But accents are just <u>one feature</u> of a dialect. You could say the words from a particular dialect in <u>any accent</u>.

People sometimes think that using a regional dialect is 'wrong' because it's not Standard English (see p. 9-11).

You say tomayto — I say tomarto...

Remember that just because people might use different grammar or different words for things, it doesn't mean what they are saying is wrong — they're just showcasing their exotic dialect.

Accent and Dialect

Accents and dialects <u>aren't fixed</u>. They're a bit like ice cream — some <u>flavours</u> are stronger than others, but you can <u>mix</u> different flavours to get something a bit different. See, just like ice cream...

Different Dialects can Merge Together

1) When different dialects or accents come into <u>contact</u> with each other, they can <u>merge together</u> and <u>become more similar</u>.

2) This is called <u>dialect levelling</u>.

3) It's happened a lot over the last 100 years, because people have been able to <u>travel</u> more and come into <u>contact</u> with people from <u>different areas</u>.

People speak Differently in Different Contexts

1) You might use a <u>different accent</u> or <u>dialect</u> depending on <u>where you are</u> or <u>who you're with</u>.

2) This is called <u>code-switching</u>.

3) A speaker might use <u>Standard English</u> to show they have a <u>high status</u>, or because it might make people think they're <u>well-educated</u>, <u>wealthy</u> and <u>intelligent</u>.

4) On the other hand, they might use a <u>regional accent</u> and <u>dialect</u> to show <u>solidarity</u> (show that they <u>fit in</u>). It could also make them seem more <u>friendly</u> and <u>down-to-earth</u>.

Rupert spoke Standard English to Lily, but never a word to anyone else.

> For example, you might use <u>Standard English</u> (see p.9) at school, and a <u>regional dialect</u> at <u>home</u>, or the other way round.

Your speech can Change because of Different Factors

You can come into <u>contact</u> with other accents and dialects in loads of ways, so the things above can happen for a <u>mixture of reasons</u>. For example:

<u>Geography</u>: You might <u>move</u> to another part of the country or go to university and come across a <u>mix of accents</u>. This might cause you to <u>change</u> your speech to <u>fit in</u>, or so you can be <u>more easily understood</u>.

<u>Media</u>: You might end up speaking in a <u>stronger</u> regional accent because you're <u>imitating people</u> off the TV.

Geography can affect speakers — closer people are louder...

Blimey. That bunch of mumbling randomers from the other side of the country seem a bit more complex than I thought, now. Well, there's plenty more where that came from...

Accent and Dialect — Worked Example

As with all of these topics, if you want to write about this in the <u>controlled assessment</u>, you're going to have to be able to <u>analyse</u> some <u>data</u>. Here's an example of the kind of things to look out for. (Have a look at p.4 if you're not sure what the numbers and symbols in the <u>transcript</u> mean.)

Geordie dialect word — you can tell that the speaker's from the Newcastle area.

Non-standard grammar is a dialect feature — plural pronoun used for the singular ('us' instead of 'me').

A: howay man pass us them will yer

B: pass yer what

A: them (.) me um (.) me (2) them (.) hoy em over

Geordie dialect word for 'throw'.

B: Aa divvent kna what yer talking about man

A: them them man (.) them (.) me tabs man (.) tabs

Geordie dialect word for 'cigarettes'.

Geordie dialect word — used to address a man or woman.

B: // aye alreet

Dialect word for 'yes'.

A: Aa couldn't remember what they were called (.) that's ridiculous that (.) just um couldn't remember like (2) hang on that's me phone (3) hello (2) yes (4) oh right (.) right I'll go and get her (2) how did she get on (4) really that's great news (3) I'll get her (1) Heather love (2) it's the people from that job (1) I'll put the kettle on (.) make her a cup of tea (.) yeh (.) OK I'll pass her over now (2) Scott man (.) sounds like Heather's got that job

Dialect feature — 'me' used instead of 'my'.

Standard English — no regional dialect features. The speaker is code-switching to Standard English, while speaking on the phone, to gain status.

B: great (.) that's great news that (1) yer a lot posher on the phone though aren't yer (.) yer voice is like (.) it's like totally different (.) yer like

A: // nah it's not (.) Aa speak the same (.) just a bit more slower

Back to using regional dialect words — the speaker's doing it for solidarity now (to fit in with his friend).

Non-standard grammar is a dialect feature — double comparative (saying 'more' and putting the '-er' on the end of the word).

B: nah it's more than that (.) yer trying to sound all posh

A: shut up man (.) will yer (.) Am gannin to make a cuppa yer want one

Geordie dialect word for 'going'.

Accent and Dialect — Practice Questions

Accents and dialects are real <u>bread-and-butter</u> stuff so make sure you can handle these questions.
If you're <u>struggling</u>, have a <u>look back</u> over the last couple of pages and then give them another go.

Q1   Which of these statements is true? Choose one answer.

    a) Accents are affected only by regional factors.
    b) Accents are variations in the words people use.
    c) Accents are variations in pronunciation.
    d) Accents are only affected by social factors.

Q2   What is a dialect?

Q3   Name two factors that can influence a person's accent.

Q4   Name three features that might differentiate one dialect from another.

Q5   What is dialect levelling?

    a) Using a different accent or dialect depending on where you are or who you're with.
    b) When accents or dialects merge together and become more similar.
    c) When you use a regional accent to show solidarity.
    d) When accents or dialects become more different.

Q6   What's it called when a speaker uses different varieties of English depending on where they are or who they're with?

Q7   What's the difference between status and solidarity in terms of how people use accent and dialect to achieve them?

Q8   How might geography affect someone's speech?

Standard English

Standard English (SE) is <u>exactly</u> what its name suggests. You should still read the page though...

Standard English *is a Social Dialect*

<u>Standard English</u> is a <u>dialect</u> of English, like <u>Cockney</u> or <u>Scouse</u>, but it <u>isn't</u> just used in one region.

1) A <u>standard</u> form of a language is the <u>representative</u> of the language. It's the variety that people think is <u>acceptable</u> or <u>correct</u> — e.g. what you look up in a <u>dictionary</u> is Standard English.

2) Standard English <u>started off</u> as the regional dialect used in the East Midlands hundreds of years ago. It gradually <u>spread</u> round the country, and became the <u>dialect</u> used in <u>print</u>.

3) It quickly became associated with <u>education</u>, <u>class</u> and <u>power</u>, rather than with a particular region.

Standard English: when you haven't got room for the full English.

This Book *is written in Standard English*

1) It's tricky to give <u>examples</u> of SE because it's what <u>other dialects</u> are normally <u>compared</u> to.

2) Think about it this way — if your language gets <u>corrected</u> at school, then that's your teacher asking you to use <u>SE</u>. It's the form of the language that seems '<u>proper</u>' or '<u>posh</u>'.

3) Here's an example of the <u>same</u> sentence written in both <u>Standard</u> and <u>non-standard</u> English:

Standard grammar — the verb agrees with the noun.

Standard English word — all English speakers would know what it means.

Standard English: Dad <u>was</u> tired because the <u>children</u> couldn't sleep.

Dialect word — speakers from different regions might not understand it.

Non-standard English: Dad <u>were</u> tired <u>coz</u> the <u>bairns</u> couldn't sleep.

Non-standard grammar — uses a different verb to agree.

Non-standard spelling.

<u>Standard English</u> is the most widely understood version of English. It's used in lots of different fields:

1) <u>Education</u> — Standard English is the variety of English taught in schools.

2) <u>Media</u> — it's used in newspapers and by newsreaders on the TV or radio.

3) <u>Formal documents</u> — it's the language used in essays, business letters and reports.

4) <u>Formal speech</u> — people use Standard English in things like public announcements.

It's tricky — but easier than studying Standard Icelandic...

Granted it's a bit of a fiddly one to get your head round at first, but all this stuff on Standard English is easy when you know how. Keep your ears open and see when you can spot it.

Received Pronunciation

Standard English is often <u>paired up</u> with a specific <u>accent</u> called <u>Received Pronunciation</u>.

Received Pronunciation is how the Queen Speaks

1) <u>Received pronunciation</u> (RP) is an <u>accent</u> that's associated with <u>Standard English</u>.

2) It gives more of a clue of someone's <u>social status</u> than about <u>where</u> they're from.

3) Most people on the <u>radio</u> and <u>TV</u> used to speak in RP, so it's sometimes called <u>BBC English</u>.

4) It's basically quite an <u>old-fashioned</u>, 'posh' accent that's gradually dying out. Not many people in the media use it any more, and the <u>Royal Family's</u> accent has changed over the years too.

Speakers might Choose to use RP or a Regional Accent

People might change their <u>accent</u> depending on <u>how</u> they want to be seen by others. You probably do this yourself <u>without</u> even <u>realising</u> it. For example:

1) Using <u>Standard English</u> and <u>RP</u> gives a person <u>overt prestige</u> — it's an <u>obvious</u> way of making themselves <u>look good</u>, because they're associated with a <u>respectable</u>, <u>educated</u>, <u>well-off</u> section of society.

2) Using a <u>regional accent</u> can give a speaker <u>covert prestige</u> — it's a <u>less obvious</u> way of making themselves look good. Rather than seeming posh, they want to come across as <u>rebellious</u> and <u>independent</u>, or <u>trustworthy</u> and <u>down-to-earth</u>.

Estuary English is Replacing RP

1) <u>Estuary English</u> is found in and around London. It borrows bits of the <u>Cockney</u> accent, but it's not as strong.

2) It's seen as a <u>trendy</u> accent in the <u>entertainment</u> industry — e.g. it's how <u>Lily Allen</u> speaks.

3) An <u>example</u> of the sorts of thing that you might spot in Estuary English is speakers replacing '<u>th</u>' sounds with '<u>f</u>' or '<u>v</u>' sounds and not pronouncing '<u>t</u>'s or '<u>l</u>'s in a standard way.

> e.g.   'My little brother's three years old.'
>
> Estuary English pronunciation
>
> would sound like 'My li-ow bruver's free years owd.'

1) Recently a new dialect called <u>Multicultural London English</u> (MLE) has emerged in the <u>London</u> area and become popular with <u>young</u> people.

2) More people are using MLE because of people in the <u>entertainment industry</u>, e.g. Dizzee Rascal.

3) It's influenced by <u>Caribbean</u>, <u>South Asian</u> and <u>West African</u> dialects, and contains lots of <u>slang</u> words like '<u>bare</u>' (very) and '<u>buff</u>' (nice).

Queen's English — but Freddie Mercury was born in Zanzibar...

Accents and dialects are really flexible. They change over time and go through phases of being popular or unpopular. Maybe my friend Adrian's squeaky yappering will be big this year...

Worked Example and Practice Questions

Have a read of this <u>wedding speech</u>, which is written in <u>Standard English</u>. I've pointed out some tasty language features for you to enjoy too. Then see how you get on with the questions.

> The speaker doesn't use any regional dialect. You can't tell where he's from or what his social background is.

> Standard vocabulary — traditional way of opening a formal speech.

> The speaker uses words like 'handsome' instead of slang terms like 'fit' or 'buff'.

> Standard grammar like 'in which we're gathered' instead of something non-standard like 'what we're gathered in'.

ladies and gentleman (.) boys and girls (1) as father of the er bride I would like to er (.) to thank you all so very much for coming here today and sharing in this (.) this wonderful occasion (.) the wedding of my dear daughter Claire and her um her handsome young groom (.) Peter (2) I'd also like to thank (.) to thank everyone who played a part in making this day so special (1) um (2) hang on (.) right (.) sorry (1) I'd er (.) first off (.) I'd like to thank er (.) Patrick (.) my er (.) my brother (.) and the rest of the um the committee of the South Riesling Cricket Club (.) for (.) for allowing us to use the this cricket field for the rather um (.) pleasant marquee in which we're gathered (2) similarly (.) I'd like to to thank my sister (.) Eileen (.) for er (.) for organising the beautiful display of er (.) of flowers that you see here today (1) one of the um (.) the ben (.) um (.) advantages of having a florist in the family (2) so (1) ladies and gentleman (.) boys and er and girls (.) I (.) I ask you to raise your glasses (2) to Claire and Peter

Q1 What is Standard English?

Q2 Name two situations where people tend to use Standard English.

Q3 Which of the sentences below is in Standard English? Choose one answer.

    a) You was trying your hardest to catch me.

    b) I've only gone and lost my rail card.

    c) Ben and Adam's well good at football.

Q4 Is Received Pronunciation a regional or social accent?

Q5 What is overt prestige?

Q6 Does using a regional dialect give people overt or covert prestige?

Slang

Slang goes <u>in</u> and <u>out of fashion</u> faster than the shoulder pad, and some of it will keep on cropping up in random places till the end of time. Much like the faithful mullet...

Slang is Informal Vocabulary

1) Slang words are <u>informal</u> and <u>colloquial</u>. People tend to use them in <u>casual speech</u>.

2) It's often <u>inventive</u> and <u>creative</u>, and enters the language in lots of different ways. For example:

> - People can give <u>new meanings</u> to <u>existing words</u> — *e.g. cool* (good).
> - <u>Existing words</u> are often <u>shortened</u> — *e.g. mare* (nightmare).
> - <u>New words</u> are <u>invented</u> — *e.g. yonks* (a long time, ages).

3) People often use slang to seem <u>rebellious</u> or <u>entertaining</u>, e.g. there's lots of slang about <u>taboo</u> subjects like <u>sex</u>, <u>sex organs</u> and <u>bodily functions</u>. Tee hee.

Slang is Specific to Certain Groups

1) Some slang words are understood pretty much <u>everywhere</u> — e.g. most <u>swear words</u>.

2) Others are <u>specific</u> to certain <u>regions</u> or <u>groups</u> (e.g. Cockney rhyming slang), so outsiders might have trouble <u>understanding</u> them.

3) People often use slang to <u>identify</u> with a particular social group — e.g. your friendship group.

4) Slang can transfer quickly between <u>cultures</u> — e.g. a lot of <u>American slang</u> has become popular in the UK, mostly through the influence of the media.

5) People often vary their slang depending on <u>who</u> they're talking to (e.g. you'd probably use less slang in a <u>job interview</u> than you would if you were just chatting with your <u>mates</u>).

6) Slang also crops up in <u>multi-modal texts</u> like <u>text messages</u> and <u>emails</u> (see section 4).

Slang is Always Changing

1) Slang words go in and out of <u>fashion</u> really <u>quickly</u>.

2) They can quickly start to sound <u>dated</u>, e.g. words like '<u>mega</u>' ('good'), or '<u>dweeb</u>' (someone who isn't cool).

3) This happens especially with <u>teenage slang</u>. When adults and younger children start using it, the slang becomes more <u>mainstream</u> and then teenagers stop using it.

Slang will come and go, but it's always good to be cool.

Slang — it's one letter away from a rude example of itself...

Cool beans. Slang constantly adapts and evolves — faster than you can say 'I think slang is pretty radical, far out, bogus, gnarley, zomba, sick, hip, bad, funky, killer-diller, heavy, stellar, tubular...'

Worked Example and Practice Questions

Here's a most enlightening <u>conversation</u> between two lovely young ladies. It's jam-packed full of <u>slang</u>, which I've helpfully pointed out for you. Once you've read it there are some questions too.

The casual language and use of slang suggest that this is a conversation between close friends of similar age.

Words from other languages may become slang terms, e.g. 'chica' is 'girl' in Spanish.

There are a lot more insults like this about women than there are for men.

'Like' is used a lot as a 'vague' filler. It suggests the speakers are quite young.

Existing word given a new meaning.

A blend word that combines 'Monday' and 'daze'.

Speaker B's interruption is supportive. She gives feedback to show that she's sympathetic.

New slang word.

Some slang words are abbreviations of existing words, e.g. this is probably short for 'confronted'.

A: hey chica (1) soz I'm late (.) I'm in a total Mondaze

B: // chill girl (.) it's no big (1) so (.) come on (.) spill

A: // oh my God (.) so it was like (.) totally bunk (.) we (.) we like rock up at the club and we're (.) he's not even got us on the (.) the guest list (.) so we're like (.) like queuing and some (.) some cow shoves past me (.) right

B: // that's so not cool

A: damn straight (.) yeah (.) proper tarty (.) really minging

B: // okay (.) so please tell me Jay at least (.) like (.) like fronted her (.) yeah

A: nah (.) that's it (.) loser couldn't take his eyes off her (1) said a girl that fine could (.) could do what she (.) what she liked

B: // ah babe (.) that sucks (1) I mean the (.) guy's fit as (.) but what a (.) a total lamester

Q1 What is slang?

Q2 Give two reasons why people might use slang.

Q3 The words below are all answers you could get if you asked someone how they are. Which of them uses slang?

    a) I'm champion.

    b) I'm very well, thanks.

    c) I'm wicked, cheers.

Q4 What types of conversation might contain lots of slang?

Q5 Why might teenage slang suddenly become unpopular with teenagers?

Sociolect

Now you've hopefully recovered from all that <u>vile</u> and <u>vulgar</u> slang, here's a lovely page all about <u>sociolect</u>... It sounds as though it should be complicated — but it's actually <u>not too tricky</u>. Honest.

Sociolect is the Language of Social Groups

1) <u>Sociolects</u> (or <u>social dialects</u>) are <u>varieties</u> of language used by particular <u>social groups</u>, e.g. middle-aged lawyers speak differently from teenagers.

2) <u>Sharing</u> a sociolect gives a group a specific <u>identity</u> — people use it to <u>fit in</u>. For example, groups of young people might speak in a sociolect that older people find <u>hard to understand</u>.

3) The <u>language</u> people use depends on different <u>social</u> factors — for example:

> • <u>Upper class</u> and <u>educated</u> people use more <u>standard forms</u> and less <u>regional dialect</u> than <u>lower class</u> people, or people who are <u>less educated</u>.
>
> • Words from <u>other languages</u> get into English because of the influence of <u>immigration</u> and <u>multiculturalism</u>. For example, <u>specialist vocab</u> from different <u>religions</u> like '<u>Ramadan</u>' and '<u>Hanukkah</u>' is used in English.

Different Jobs have their own Sociolect

1) <u>Occupational sociolect</u> is the <u>distinctive language</u> used by people who do <u>particular jobs</u>, e.g. <u>train drivers</u> use different words at work than <u>nurses</u>.

2) It makes communicating at work <u>quicker</u> and more <u>precise</u>.

3) It's made up of <u>jargon</u> — <u>specialist terms</u> that people who don't do the job might not understand. E.g. words in an <u>electrician's</u> sociolect might be 'transformer', 'faceplate', 'fuse', 'amp', 'earth'. It's used for a <u>specific purpose</u>, so it's not everyday language.

4) Sometimes people use jargon to <u>confuse</u>, <u>exclude</u> or <u>impress</u> people who <u>aren't experts</u>.

Sociolect could be Influenced by Gender

1) It's thought that <u>women</u> are more <u>supportive</u> in conversations than men, e.g. men tend to interrupt more.

2) Studies have shown that <u>women</u> use more <u>standard forms</u> than men — they want <u>overt prestige</u> (see p. 10). They also <u>swear less</u> than men.

3) It seems that <u>male</u> sociolects contain more <u>non-standard grammar</u> and men are more likely to have stronger <u>regional accents</u> — to get <u>covert prestige</u> (see p. 10).

> [IMPORTANT POINT]
> These are all generalisations. You might have noticed that lots of men and women don't fit in with these findings, so you should bear in mind that gender is only one factor that can influence speech.

What's the difference between sociolects and socialists?...

This stuff on sociolects might seem as useful as an underwater-towel, but you'll pick up marks if you know about it in your English GCSE. It really is important, so get your geek on and learn it.

Sociolect

Sociolect part deux. It'll be really useful to know about sociolect for your <u>GCSE</u>, and luckily for you, you're on <u>exactly</u> the right page to find out the rest of it. Coincidence? Or fate...

Multi-Modal Texts can have their own Sociolect

1) Sociolects can come through in <u>multi-modal</u> texts (see section 4), like <u>text messages</u>, <u>emails</u> and <u>instant messenger conversations</u>.

2) This is because people often write in the <u>same</u> way that they <u>talk</u> when they're <u>texting</u> or <u>emailing</u>.

3) For example, they might use the <u>slang</u> words that are going round their <u>school</u> at the time, or use <u>occupational jargon</u> in a <u>work email</u>.

4) This means you can sometimes tell just as much about someone's <u>social</u> background from an <u>email</u> they've sent as from hearing them have a <u>conversation</u>.

Niall was ready to show the world his complex sociolect — right after he completed level six...

Language Changes depending on Context

1) It's important to remember that <u>sociolects</u> are features of <u>group language</u>.

2) <u>Individual speakers</u> use <u>different sociolects</u> depending on <u>who</u> they're talking to.

3) For example, when they're <u>not at work</u>, <u>doctors</u> will speak in a completely <u>different sociolect</u> to the one they use when they're talking to <u>other medical professionals</u>.

You might find that the way you speak <u>changes</u> depending on:

- Who you're with — e.g. the language you use with a <u>brother</u> or <u>sister</u> might contain slang that your <u>parents</u> don't understand.

- Where you are — e.g. if you're at a <u>football match</u> you'd probably use words like 'Ref!' and 'offside!' that you wouldn't use if you were at the <u>cinema</u>.

- What you're doing — e.g. if you're <u>giving a speech</u> at school you might use more <u>standard forms</u> because you're in a <u>formal context</u>.

Using the right '<u>type</u>' of language in <u>different contexts</u> is really important for making yourself understood. E.g. if the <u>newsagent</u> told you to '<u>open wide</u>', you'd think it was pretty <u>weird</u>, but you wouldn't think it was weird at the <u>dentist's</u>...

...if you write about sociolects you'll get more Marx...

Cringe. I'm sorry but it had to be done... Anyhoo, there's a handy worked example on the next page and a few practice questions to have a look at too. I really am too good to you.

Worked Example and Practice Questions

If you've read the last couple of pages, you should now be an expert in <u>sociolect</u>. Make sure you know what it's all about by reading this <u>worked example</u> then having a bash at the <u>questions</u>.

Occupational sociolect — jargon words associated with fitness and training.

The speakers use informal language to gain covert prestige.

Informal, friendly address term, usually used in conversations between men.

Speaker A interrupts speaker B to control the conversation.

Speaker B's occupational sociolect is different from speaker A's.

Jargon. This is a blend word that combines 'boxing' and 'exercise'.

A: right (.) it depends on what kind of exercise you're looking for (1) spinning's a er great workout but it's pretty intense

B: yeah (.) I'm a bit out of of shape (.) I'd better start off gentle

A: what d'you do for a living mate

B: // I'm a er (.) landscape gardener (1) water features and that (.) y'know

A: // cool (1) must keep you pretty fit (.) yeah

B: used to (.) yeah (.) I'm more on the design side now though (1) where would you like your sun terrace (.) madam (1)

A: // haha (.) yeah (.)

B: // know what I mean

A: yeah (.) well (.) no worries mate (.) we can sort you out (1) I reckon you should start off with boxercise (1) it's great for cardio

---

Q1   What is sociolect?

Q2   True or false? Sociolects can reinforce group identities.

Q3   Give an example of a group that might have its own sociolect.

Q4   What sort of sociolect might contain lots of specialist language and jargon?

Q5   Apart from in spoken language, where else might sociolect crop up?

Idiolect

It's <u>really important</u> to know about <u>idiolects</u> for your GCSE. You'll need to think about how <u>all</u> the little <u>bits and bobs</u> that have come up so far form how <u>one person</u> speaks.

Idiolect is the Unique Language of an Individual

1) The <u>word choices</u> people make, and the <u>way</u> they <u>form sentences</u>, are <u>specific</u> to them.

2) This means that the way you use language can be a big part of your <u>identity</u>.

3) Your individual way of speaking is called your <u>idiolect</u>. It's basically the <u>unique combination</u> of all the different <u>varieties</u> of speech covered in this section, that makes your speech <u>yours</u>.

Idiolect is Influenced by Where You're From...

1) Your <u>accent</u> and <u>dialect</u> form part of your <u>idiolect</u> (see p.5-6).

2) For example, if you're from Plymouth then you might have a West Country <u>accent</u> and use <u>dialect</u> words, like 'bock' for 'mess up'.

3) But not everyone from the same <u>area</u> speaks in exactly the <u>same</u> way. E.g. You might have <u>moved</u> from somewhere else and kept some aspects of your <u>other</u> regional accent and dialect, while picking up bits of the Plymouth one. This way of speaking will be <u>unique</u> to you.

...your Age...

1) People of <u>different ages</u> tend to use <u>different language</u>. You'll probably have noticed that your <u>teachers</u> and <u>parents</u> don't talk in the same way or use the same words as your <u>friends</u>.

2) A lot of <u>young people</u> use more '<u>vague</u>' language (e.g. '<u>like</u>' and '<u>sort of</u>') than older people.

3) For example, you probably won't hear your grandad saying *and it was like really awful cos I turned to him and was like "leave me alone" and he was like "no way"*...

...and your Sociolect

1) The way you speak is <u>influenced</u> by all the different <u>sociolects</u> you use.

2) No-one is <u>just</u> middle class or a teenager or whatever — everyone's a <u>mixture</u> of all of these things.

3) This means that your <u>idiolect</u> is the <u>product</u> of all these different <u>factors</u> mixed together.

4) It also <u>changes</u> all the time depending on the <u>context</u> you're in — e.g. you might speak differently to your boss than you do to a friend. This is your <u>unique verbal repertoire</u>.

Kenneth's idiolect was calm, soft and strangely flirtatious.

Lloyd Grossman — now that's an interesting idiolect...

Your idiolect is basically the result of everything that makes you talk in the way that you do. If you're not too sure about it, have a look at the worked example and questions on the next page.

Worked Example and Practice Questions

Have a look at the <u>idiolect features</u> picked out in this worked example, and then try the questions.

Slang word for 'really' or 'very' — giving an existing word a new meaning.

West Midlands dialect word for 'good'. The speaker might be from that region, or picked up dialect from it somehow.

'Settee' is sometimes seen as a 'lower class' word to use than 'sofa', so it could hint at the speaker's social background.

Regional dialect differences — speaker A uses 'pants' to mean 'underpants', speaker B uses it to mean 'trousers'.

Using 'like' as a 'vague' filler suggests the speaker is quite young.

Non-standard grammar (Standard English would be 'sitting'). This could show the speaker's regional or social background.

Non-standard word for 'something' — used in lots of dialects. It suggests the speaker is in an informal setting.

Slang words that could be unique to the speaker, or part of their sociolect with their friends.

A: so he says like (.) like he says he's planned this romantic thing for em for valentine's right (.) like proper bostin thing for em to do once he clocked off at erm like seven or whatever it was

B: yeh he said he was gonna pick her up

A: yeh right so then like then (.) like she gets home at half past and he's just sat there in his pants on the settee (1) asleep (.) telly blaring on watching some antiques thing or summat

B: // in his pants

A: ah right yeh I mean like (.) like in his boxers (.) not his trousers like (.) and he's all

B: I was gonna say what's wrong with being in yer pants

A: // anyway she was so vexed she hit him on the head with the doofer

Q1   What is idiolect?

a)   The unique language of a social group.

b)   The unique language of a geographical region.

c)   The unique language of an individual speaker.

Q2   As well as geographical and social factors, what else can influence a speaker's idiolect?

Q3   Which of these statements is true?

a)   Your idiolect is part of your sociolect.

b)   Sociolect can be part of your idiolect.

c)   Idiolect and sociolect are different words for the same thing.

Social Attitudes to Spoken Language

The way people speak affects what other people think about them.
People form opinions about others based on how they talk <u>all the time</u> without even realising.

People have Different Attitudes towards Standard English

1) Some people see <u>Standard English</u> as the '<u>correct</u>' or '<u>pure</u>' form of the language.
   Their view is that using another dialect, e.g. a regional dialect, isn't using English '<u>properly</u>'.

2) They might worry about <u>text-speak</u> in multi-modal texts like <u>emails</u> and <u>text messages</u> (see section 4) because they say that young people will end up with a poor knowledge of '<u>correct</u>' English.

3) Other people argue that language is <u>always changing</u> and that all varieties of English should be <u>valued equally</u>.

4) Whether it's <u>appropriate</u> to use non-standard English depends on <u>context</u>. You'd probably use more Standard English if you were giving a <u>speech</u> at school, than you would just talking to your <u>friends</u>.

Terry had a unique way of showing his own social attitudes.

You might Judge people because of their Accent and Dialect

People make judgements about someone's <u>background</u> and <u>education</u> based on how they speak, e.g.

1) People from the <u>north</u> of England often think that people with <u>southern accents</u> sound '<u>posh</u>'.

2) Some people <u>assume</u> that people who use <u>regional dialects</u> are <u>uneducated</u> or <u>lower class</u>.

3) On the other hand, <u>regional varieties</u> of English can be seen as more <u>down-to-earth</u> and <u>modest</u>
   — you might think someone's being fancy or fake if they try and <u>change</u> their <u>regional accent</u>.

> For example, some companies deliberately put their <u>call centres</u> in places where people tend to have <u>strong regional accents</u>, like <u>Merseyside</u>, so their staff seem <u>friendly</u> and <u>approachable</u> to customers on the phone.

Some people think Slang is Incorrect English

<u>Slang</u> is often seen as being too <u>informal</u> to use in certain situations.

1) Some people worry that slang doesn't follow the 'proper' <u>spelling</u> and <u>grammar rules</u> of <u>Standard English</u>.

2) They think that if you use slang you're <u>lowering standards</u>, and assume that people who use lots of slang are lower class and uneducated.

3) Slang is seen as the language of <u>informal speech</u>, so it's not thought of as <u>appropriate</u> to use in a <u>formal context</u>, e.g. you'd lose marks if you wrote an essay using slang words and phrases.

I don't like your attitude, young lady...

Spoken language is something you'll come across every day including the day of your GCSE, so make sure you know what other people think about it and can talk about their different opinions.

Worked Example

This is the <u>mother of all examples</u>. The next <u>four pages</u> cover examples and questions for everything in Section Two. Dialects, slang, idiolect — the lot. So, deep breath, and here we go...

> A: so where does it hurt exactly
>
> B: I think it's one of me (1) me back teeth (2) this side.
>
> A: // I expect it's a molar (1) when did you last have a check-up
>
> B: can't member (3) bout (.) er (.) bout a year ago (.) just before we was (.) yeah cos we was (.) going away like
>
> A: well (.) I'll sort this out for you now (6) looks like you'll be needing a (.) a filling and then you'll need to book in for a proper check-up (1) make a (.) an um (.) appointment before you leave today (.) won't you
>
> B: // okicoki
>
> A: I'll just give you a little injection (.) numb the pain (1) or would you prefer without
>
> B: well (1) I (.) er (.) I think you'd best give us a jab (1) if (.) if it's gonna hurt like
>
> A: o(.)kay (2) just hold still for a jiffy and (3) there we go (1) just give that a (.) second to work (5) can you feel (1) that
>
> B: that's (.) yeah (1) nothing (2) let's geddit over with doc
>
> A: great (2) now (.) just relax (1) you might feel a slight (.) pressure but it ( ) it won't hurt a bit

Annotations:

- Non-standard grammar — 'me' used instead of 'my'.
- Occupational sociolect associated with dentistry.
- Missing out the first syllable is probably a feature of the speaker's idiolect.
- A feature of the speaker's idiolect, meaning 'OK'.
- Slang term for 'injection'.
- Informal slang — suggests that the speaker might have a lower status than the dentist.
- The dentist starts the conversation by asking a question, showing power in the conversation.
- The dentist uses Standard English, which gives overt prestige and shows status.
- Non-standard grammar. In Standard English it would be 'we were'.
- Occupational sociolect — jargon word associated with dentistry.
- Dialect feature, use of plural instead of singular pronoun ('us' instead of 'me').
- Slang and maybe a feature of the speaker's idiolect.
- Elision — merging of two words ('get it') into one.
- Imperative (command) — shows the dentist has the power to tell the patient what to do.

Worked Example

Now have a look at this little lot. By the end of this page you'll be a <u>spoken language machine</u>, able to take over the linguistic world and rule with your mighty tongue. (Small print: this may not actually happen.)

> Phatic language (small talk).

A: Mrs Trafford (.) how are you today (.) sorry to have kept you (1) we've been rushed off our feet all morning (2) now then (.) what can I do you for

> Non-standard English — maybe a dialect feature. In standard English it would be 'what can I do for you'.

B: well (.) I'd like the (.) the back left long (.) but I think perhaps some layers at the top

> Occupational sociolect — jargon word associated with hairdressing.

A: no probs Mrs T. (1) looks like you've got a (.) a few split ends here at the back

> Speaker B is addressed quite formally, but speaker A is addressed informally, showing that speaker B has more power in the relationship.

> Slang word, usually associated with middle-class speakers.

B: // oh crikey (1) how awful (1) well just (.) just do as you think best Sandra (1) but not too short or I shan't be able to tie it back

A: that's fine Mrs T. (.) see what I can do for you (2) you off out tonight then (1) are you

> Ellipsis — speaker A skips the first word of sentences. This might be an idiolect feature.

B: // yes (.) my husband's taking me to that (.) you know that new Italian restaurant in town

A: oooh fancy (1) better get you glammed up then hadn't we (.) you got a nice dress picked out then have you

> Tag question — the question's 'tagged on' to the end of the sentence. This is a politeness strategy to keep the conversation going.

> Slang word, abbreviation of 'casual' and maybe a feature of the speaker's idiolect.

B: oh I thought smart cas you know (.) although I did (.) I must admit I did buy a new (.) oh what's it called (1) gosh how silly (1) you know (.) a (.) a dooberry haha (1) goes round your neck

> Slang word, possibly a feature of the speaker's idiolect.

A: a (.) like a (.) scarf you mean

B: // no a (1) well sort of (.) yes (1) a (1) a (.) pashmina that's it (1) gosh I'm losing my marbles today Sandra

> Idiolect or sociolect feature. Speaker B uses a lot of exclamations of surprise — e.g. 'gosh', 'crikey'.

A: hahaha (1) wouldn't worry Mrs T. (1) happens to me all the time

Practice Example

Have a go at the <u>questions</u> that go with this extract and see how you get on.

1) Why do you think speaker A uses Standard English?

A: Lynch (1) Woodley (1) take a seat (.) I think you know why er (.) why Miss Turnbull sent you to me (3) well

B: yes (.) yes sir

C: // yeah

A: yes sir (.) Lynch (.) not yeah

C: // yes (.) sir

The practice examples in the book have been chosen to show specific language features — but remember that they also contain lots of features that haven't been highlighted too.

2) Is this standard or non-standard grammar?

A: can you explain your (.) your actions

C: it were a joke (1) sir (.) we never thought she'd like start up like (.) like blubbing

A: it (.) was (.) a (.) joke (1) a joke (1) perhaps you'd find it (1) amusing if I locked you in a store cupboard (.) eh Lynch (3) answer me boy

C: // not really (.) sir

6) Why might speaker B change his grammar from standard to non-standard here?

A: no (.) I rather thought not (1) and you Woodley (.) I'd thought better of you (.) anything you'd like to add

B: it was a (.) it were a joke (.) sir (1) like (.) like what Simon said (.) then we (.) we went to let her out and she was (.) she were in a (.) a proper state

8) Why do you think speaker A addresses speaker B by his first name here?

A: hmmm (1) wait outside Lynch (.) I want to talk to Woodley for a moment (5) anything else you'd like to share (.) Josh

3) What's this an example of?

4) What is this word an example of?

5) What do these address terms tell you about the relationship between the speakers?

7) What's this an example of?

9) Write a mini-essay where you analyse the language features in this extract. You don't just have to focus on the features that have been highlighted in the blue boxes.

Practice Example

Finally, it's the end of the <u>mammoth</u> Section Two. Strap yourself in for the last lot of <u>questions</u>...

1) Explain how the structure of the conversation suggests that it is an interview.

A: now then er (1) Zoe (.) what experience have you had of working in a restaurant

2) Is this formal or informal language?

B: well I (.) um (.) I worked down (.) down Burgerville Saturdays

A: // yes (1) well I

3) Why do you think the speaker apologises here?

B: // when I were (.) sorry (.) when I were at school

4) Why might speaker A be using Standard English?

A: I er (.) wouldn't quite class Burgerville as a restaurant Zoe though it's all (.) er (1) valuable experience (2) what about silver service

5) What is this phrase an example of?

B: well (.) I um I done some waitressing last year in a café (1) that were good that were (1) being busy y'know (.) I don't like sort of standing round too much (1) I done some shop work once and it were right boring

A: we might be able to use you in the kitchen (1) have you had er much much experience with preparing food

6) What's this?

B: aye I do (.) I like cooking (1) it were me best subject at school (1) me ma hates cooking owt so I get the tea most nights (1) I done some right swanky stuff

7) Is this standard or non-standard grammar?

8) What is this word an example of?

A: that's great Zoe (2) so the er (.) the kitchen can get very busy (.) how well do you (.) would you say you cope under pressure

9) What's this?

10) What's this an example of?

B: all right (.) yeah (.) I mean I (.) I do get sorta (.) mithered a bit sometimes when I don't know how to (.) how to do summat (1) summat new (.) y'know

11) Write a mini-essay where you analyse the language features in this extract. You don't just have to focus on the features that have been highlighted in the blue boxes.

Public Talk

People use language differently in <u>speeches</u> or <u>presentations</u> to how they <u>chat</u> with their friends.

Public Speech is usually quite Formal

Public talk is the kind of language that's <u>written down</u> to be <u>spoken</u>. It could be things like:

- a <u>speech</u> in your <u>school assembly</u>
- a <u>presentation</u> to your <u>class</u>
- a <u>politician's</u> election address
- a <u>police officer</u> giving a <u>statement</u> on the news

1) Public speakers often use <u>Standard English</u>. This makes their speech sound <u>formal</u>.

2) They generally avoid using <u>slang</u> so the audience is more likely to take them <u>seriously</u>.

3) Public speaking can be used to <u>influence</u> people or <u>persuade</u> the audience.

4) Speakers usually <u>prepare</u> what they're going to say to avoid <u>stumbling</u> or <u>unintentional pauses</u>.

5) They <u>don't</u> usually expect <u>interaction</u> in the same way you would in a <u>conversation</u> — although in some situations there might be a structured time for the audience to <u>ask questions</u>.

How you say things can Change the Meaning

These <u>paralinguistic features</u> (see p.3) can help speakers <u>connect</u> with the audience:

1) <u>Pauses</u> — Pauses can be used for <u>effect</u>, and to help give the speech <u>structure</u>.

2) <u>Tone</u> — Tone of voice can show how a person <u>feels</u>, e.g. angry, sarcastic.

3) <u>Stress</u> — Emphasising certain words will make them <u>stand out</u>.

4) <u>Rhythm</u> — Language techniques like <u>three part lists</u>, e.g. 'He's ugly, stupid and rude' and <u>repetition</u> can give speeches rhythm and help them build to a <u>climax</u>.

5) <u>Gestures</u> — You can make a point more <u>forceful</u> by doing things like <u>banging your fist</u>.

6) <u>Eye contact</u> — Speakers try to <u>engage</u> their audience by looking at them <u>directly</u>.

7) <u>Volume</u> — Speakers with loud voices can seem more <u>confident</u>, <u>excited</u> or <u>angry</u>.

8) <u>Pace</u> — Slow speech makes the speaker sound <u>calm</u> and in <u>control</u>.

Public talk is written to Suit the Audience

1) Just like with everything in this book, <u>public talk</u> is different in different <u>contexts</u>.

2) For example, in a talk at a <u>primary school assembly</u>, a speaker would probably use <u>easy words</u>, <u>short sentences</u> and lots of <u>eye contact</u> and <u>hand gestures</u>. They might use things like <u>alliteration</u>, speak <u>slowly</u> and put lots of <u>emphasis</u> on descriptive words — e.g. 'the <u>biiiiiiiiiiiiiiig</u> balloon <u>burst</u> with a great <u>big</u> BANG!'

3) You <u>wouldn't</u> expect speech like this for an <u>adult audience</u>, e.g in a <u>political debate</u>.

I've got hair in strange new places — wait, that's pubic talk...

Websites like YouTube or BBC iPlayer contain loads of examples of public speaking. Listen to a few and pick out what the speakers say and do to make their speeches so incredibly gripping.

Public Talk — Worked Example

That's all very well, I hear you cry, but what does it all mean... Never fear, my eager young friend. Here's a lovely <u>worked example</u> of a written down <u>public speech</u> (rather than a transcript of one).

> Colleagues, trusted advisers, (pause, look up) *friends*.
>
> I stand before you today as a humble man. Humbled by the great honour bestowed upon me as leader of this proud party. Humbled by the confidence in me you have shown throughout this most challenging of campaigns. Humbled by the great moral duty you have entrusted me with as the new Prime Minister of this our beloved country. (Pause)
>
> And yes (nod), I also stand before you today as a proud man. Proud to be of service to my party. Proud to be of service to my community. Proud to be of service to my country.
>
> And to do that well, I need your help. Without you, I am nothing. Without you, the party is nothing. Without you, *this country* is nothing. (Pause)
>
> We must work together. There are storms ahead. Dark days in store. The road to prosperity will not be a smooth one. But we are strong. This is why the people have put their trust in us. They know that no matter what trials and tribulations lie ahead, we can deliver. And that's what we have promised. *DELIVERANCE.* (Pause)
>
> But deliverance from what?
>
> Deliverance from *poverty*, from *uncertainty* and most of all from *fear*.
>
> We are a party of promise – but not empty promises, my friends. No, no. We are a party that promises to deliver and yes, colleagues, friends, *deliver we shall*!

The speech is written in Standard English with no regional dialect features. This shows that the context and audience are formal.

Eye contact helps the speaker engage with the audience. It also emphasises the word 'friends'.

Body language / gesture helps to emphasise the point.

Pause slows down the pace to build a sense of anticipation.

Repetition.

This speech is very rhythmic, with lots of repetition. This allows the speaker to emphasise key points.

This word is louder to emphasise it.

Three-part list helps to put the emphasis on the final word.

The speaker stresses these words so they stand out as the most important and give a rousing conclusion to the speech.

SECTION THREE — SPOKEN GENRES

Public Talk — Practice Questions

Righty-ho. Here's a chance to see if you've been taking in any of the information on the last couple of pages — or if you've just been gazing at the page and daydreaming about your tea...

Q1   What dialect might public speakers use to sound formal?

Q2   Why might public speakers avoid using slang?

Q3   How can tone of voice change the meaning of what you're saying?

Q4   How might a speaker use hand gestures to help get their point across?

Q5   Why would a speaker make eye contact with the audience?

Q6   Outline three things that a speaker might do to tailor their speech to a formal adult audience.

Public Talk — Practice Example

There, that wasn't too painful was it... Sadly there comes a time in everyone's life when the <u>language features</u> aren't written in for you and you have to <u>think them up yourself</u>.

1) Is the style of address formal or informal?

2) Why does the speaker pause here?

4) Look at the initial sounds of 'dawn' and 'dusk'. What is this an example of?

6) How does this affect the pace of the speech?

8) Is the speaker using Standard English? Why / why not?

good morning pupils of Haverstone High School (1) teachers (.) Headmistress (1) can I first thank you so much for inviting me here today to tell you about the charity I represent (1) Right On (1) as some of you might already know (.) Right On is a charity that seeks to promote the rights of children not just in this country but also in other (.) less prosperous parts of the world (1) so what are children's rights (1) here are just a few (2) the right to feel safe and secure (2) the right to go to school (2) the right to freedom of expression (2) the right to health and social care (2) the right to a caring and supportive environment (2) how often are these rights ignored (1) in some countries (.) there are children who work from dawn to dusk (1) some in fields (1) some in factories (1) some down mines (1) some of these children are as young as five years old (1) they have no time for play (.) no time for school (.) no time for sleep (1) they live in darkness and misery (1) the work they do affects their health (1) some of them die (3) how does this happen (2) it happens because some people are greedy (1) they pay low wages so that they can make bigger profits (.) even if it means that children are abused and exploited (1) indeed some large corporations in the West have benefited from this exploitation (.) ignoring the true facts of child labour (2) Right On seeks to put an end to such practices by promoting children's rights (1) we do this through advertising (.) through publicity campaigns and (.) of course (.) like today (.) by talking to people (1) if you would like to find out more (.) please ask for one of our leaflets which you can get from your teachers (1) in there you will find information about different ways you can make a difference (2) thank you for listening

3) How would you describe what's going on here?

5) How does the speaker create rhythm here?

7) How do you think the speaker might say these words? Why?

9) What effect does addressing the audience have here?

10) Write a mini-essay where you analyse the language features in this extract. You don't just have to focus on the features that have been highlighted in the blue boxes.

TV and Radio

TV and radio are both riddled with spoken language so they can be great resources for your study.

There are Lots of Different Types of Spoken Language in the Media

1) Some spoken language on the TV and radio is written to be spoken. E.g. news reports are carefully structured using things like headlines, details and quotes, to get the story across clearly.

2) It can also be spontaneous — e.g. conversations on reality shows.

3) In informative programs, like the news and documentaries, people often use Standard English.

4) Radio plays and TV soaps and dramas mimic spontaneous conversations. Regional dialects are often used and the character's age and background is shown through their speech. They also include features like interruption, overlap and fillers to make the dialogue seem more realistic.

5) Speech that's scripted to sound like real-life talk is never exactly like a real spontaneous conversation. If it was then it wouldn't flow, and the audience might miss bits because people were talking over each other too much. Here's an example from a TV soap opera script:

> Vicky's interrupted, but the audience hears enough to know what her next word will be, so the meaning isn't lost.

Vicky:	Hey! (*she pauses*) What's your prob-
Saul:	(*interrupting*) What's it to you, eh? (*he pauses*) It's not like you ever gave a damn about my feelings before.
Vicky:	That ain't true. (*softly*) Look, babe, it's only cos I wanna help.
Saul:	Yeah? (*angrily*) Well you can help by staying away from me.

> Tag question.

> Words are slurred together (elision) to make the speakers sound more natural.

Radio Language is Different from TV Language

1) TV language has pictures, gestures and facial expressions, and sometimes text to help get the meaning across.

2) This means that TV presenters can take long pauses and use deixis (e.g. point to something and call it 'that', see p.4).

3) On the radio there are no visual clues. Everything has to be explained, so radio presenters are more likely to use full sentences than TV presenters.

4) Radio presenters have to fill silences, so they can't afford to pause very much.

After 18 hours, Kirsty began to wonder whether she was taking her English homework too seriously.

Broadcasting Language is Always Changing

1) Back in the day, everyone on the TV and radio used to talk in Standard English with an RP accent — this is why it's also known as 'BBC English' (see p.10).

2) Nowadays regional accents are used in lots of different types of broadcast. Newsreaders and presenters come from a much wider range of social, regional and cultural backgrounds, which reflects the cultural diversity of the country.

3) People also often mimic the way people speak on TV — it becomes part of their idiolect.

Actually, Mum, it's for my English project...

This isn't just an opportunity to sit in front of the telly with a clipboard. You've actually got to think really carefully about the spoken language used (make sure you explain this bit to your parents).

TV and Radio — Worked Example

Make sure you've got all that in your noggin by having a read of the worked examples on the next two pages — this one's a transcript of a TV news report.

The speech is very fluent, with no fillers. This is because it's prepared.

Complex sentences in Standard English are used for the main report.

Pauses are used to make sure that complex sentences make sense.

Convention of TV news broadcasts.

Speaker A uses a respectful address term for the guest to show their high status.

Formal greeting in Standard English. There's no regional dialect or slang used.

Headlines use incomplete sentences and relatively long pauses as pictures are displayed — this gets across the most important information and encourages viewers to keep watching.

Deictic language — relies on the viewer being able to see what's being referred to.

Linking phrases are used to structure the report and make it clear that this is a different story.

Each new speaker is introduced to make the report more fluid and easier to follow.

A: good evening and welcome to the six o'clock news (.) I'm Amita Dhimar (1) tonight's headlines (1) kidnapped property developer released unharmed (2) health fears over new celebrity detox (2) petrol prices set to rise to unprecedented levels (2) early success for British players at the US Open (2) tonight's top story (.) Peter Wilkinson (.) the forty-two year old multimillionaire property developer (.) kidnapped three days ago (.) has been released unharmed (1) Mr Wilkinson was seized at gunpoint on Friday evening as he returned from a night out with his wife (1) David Willets reports

B: Mr Wilkinson was found earlier today (.) in this underground car park in Bexton (1) he was bound and gagged (.) but otherwise unharmed (1) why he was taken (.) and whether a ransom had been paid for his safe return (.) is still uncertain (1) what we do know is that Mr Wilkinson has been reunited with his family (.) in hospital (.) where he's being treated for mild dehydration (.) the family have requested privacy until Mr Wilkinson is fully recovered from his ordeal (1) police are continuing with their investigations (1) this is David Willets (.) in Bexton (.) for Planet News (1) back to Amita in the studio

A: thanks David (1) in other news (1) a new detox diet (.) endorsed by celebrities including singer Mina Hurst and model Letitia Barden (.) has been criticised by health experts as barbaric and dangerous (1) dieters are encouraged to stop eating altogether for three days (.) and to drink only water (1) I'm joined now by Doctor Marcus Trievnor from the National Diet and Nutrition Authority (1) Doctor Trievnor (.) welcome

C: good evening (.) Amita

SECTION THREE — SPOKEN GENRES

TV and Radio — Worked Example

If you've just come from page 29, you'll have seen a fabulous <u>transcript</u> of a TV news report. This is the same kind of thing, but for a local <u>radio</u> station. Whilst you're reading, have a think about the <u>differences</u> between the two reports — the comments down the side should get you started.

Less formal language than on TV example — trying to create a 'chatty' tone.

Fillers are used to prevent long pauses — this is a non-fluency feature.

All sentences are complete and in Standard English.

Speaker corrects himself — this is a non-fluency feature.

Making jokes and laughing makes the report less formal and more chatty.

Emotive slang word, which grabs the audience's attention.

Speaker introduces who the new voice will belong to and tells them when to speak.

Pauses are very short because the listener would lose interest if there were long silences.

The speaker addresses the audience directly — this makes the speech seem less formal and more friendly.

Filler. This makes the report seem more informal and less scripted.

Repetition — speaker repeats word rather than leaving a long silence.

Speaker B makes it clear that he's finished talking, so speaker A can take over.

A: we'll be back after the er the news with this week's number one (1) Rhys (.) what's going on in the world

B: hi Craig (.) yeah it's been a (.) a busy day for news (1) our top story is that local multimillionaire Peter (.) er Wilkinson (.) who was (.) you'll remember he was kidnapped at gunpoint on er (.) on Monday evening has been found alive and well in an underground car-park (.) there's still no indication of why he was kidnapped in the first place or whether a (.) a er (.) ransom's been paid (.) police have issued a statement requesting privacy for Peter and his family for the (.) for the time being (.) well Pete (.) it's good to have you back and our thoughts are with you mate (.) in other news petrol prices are on the up again (.) they're predicted to hit an all time high later this week (.) well (.) luckily I can walk to work (.) but if you (.) if you're going to be (.) or or if you've been affected (.) by this then give us a call

A: shocking (.) isn't it mate

B: yeah (.) if it keeps up you're gonna have to (.) to sell your Jag [laughs] (1) anyway (.) let us know what er what you think (.) our (.) the other top story today is about this new er celebrity celebrity detox diet (.) manufacturers claim it can help you lose up to a stone in two er two weeks (.) but today experts have (.) have slammed the diet (.) saying that it (.) it's dangerous and could cause long term health problems for dieters (1) there'll be more from me at midday

A: thanks Rhys (.) I don't hold with all these fad diets myself (.) get your running shoes on people and (.) enjoy the the lovely weather

TV and Radio — Practice Questions

Have a crack at these practice questions — painstakingly crafted by a team of experts to test your knowledge, intelligence and endurance, and push your performance to the limit. There, I tried to make it sound exciting — but whether you fell for it or not — you should probably just do them.

Q1   Why do news bulletins use headlines?

Q2   Is Standard English more likely to be used for a documentary or a radio play?

Q3   Describe two ways that scripted speech can be made to sound natural.

Q4   Read this extract from a live commentary of a football match.

> here's Saha making space along the left hand side (1)
> Cowley in support to his right (1) cross hit hard and
> low (.) Robinson picks it up on the far right side by the
> corner flag (.) cuts inside (.) passes to Burton

    a)   Do you think this was broadcast on the TV or the radio?

    b)   How can you tell?

Q5   Explain how broadcasting language shows cultural diversity.

TV and Radio — Practice Example

What's even better than listening to top Radio DJs yappering on? Reading them yapper on and <u>answering questions</u> on what they say... So here's a whole page for you to get stuck in to. Enjoy.

1) What's this?

RADIO PRESENTER:

so (.) here we go (.) it's erm five past nine and you're listening to Radio Lynx FM (1) my name's Larry Longton (.) and I'll be taking you all the way through to twelve o clock midday (.) playing you the very best hits around (1) but first the weather (1) well (.) erm (.) guess what (.) it's gonna be cold and rainy (1) nothing new there folks (1) after all (.) it is summer (.) so (.) let's think of ways to cheer ourselves up (1) here's an idea (.) why don't you take your grandmother to the shops (1) and see how much you get for her [laughs] (1) only joking all you grannies out there (1) my grandmother's eighty-nine and I love her (1) aren't grandmothers lovely (1) now, a few words of wisdom for you (1) he who drinks from the sea of lurve will never be thirsty (1) I like that (1) lurve (.) lurve (.) lurve (.) OK (.) enough frivolity (.) let's get serious for a moment (1) let's bring it down (1) later in the programme I'll be joined by er Holly Crowland (.) now Holly is president of Youth Against Ageism (.) an organisation that seeks to seeks to challenge all forms of discrimination based on age (1) you know (.) we think that ageism only relates to older people (.) but it can be directed against younger people too (1) you can get married (.) with your parent's consent (.) at sixteen but you can't vote (1) is this right my friends (.) the minimum pay for sixteen and seventeen year olds is set lower (.) than it is for eighteens and over (.) is this fair (2) it don't don't seem very fair to me (1) let's hear what Holly has to say

2) What's this an example of?

3) What could you say about this word?

4) What do you notice about the pauses in this transcript?

5) What's this?

6) What kind of non-fluency feature is this?

7) How does the presenter try to involve the audience here?

8) Is this standard or non-standard grammar?

9) Write a mini-essay where you analyse the language features in this extract. You don't just have to focus on the features that have been highlighted in the blue boxes.

Modes

In the good old days, language was either <u>written</u> or <u>spoken</u>... sadly for you, we live in a time where there's a weird 'hybrid genre' that you have to learn about — <u>multi-modal talk</u>.

Written Language is often Formal

1) Written language includes letters, essays, novels, recipes and reports.

2) In <u>written</u> modes the <u>words</u> have to make the <u>meaning</u> clear, because you <u>can't</u> see or hear any <u>paralinguistic features</u> (e.g. facial expression or gestures).

3) Writers might try to get across features of <u>spoken language</u>, like <u>stress</u> and <u>tone</u>. They do this by using things like:

> * <u>underlining</u>
> * *italics*
> * CAPITALISATION
> * punctuation....!!??!

 This is called <u>sound representation</u>.

Spoken Modes include Paralinguistic Features

1) Speakers use things like <u>stress</u>, <u>volume</u> and <u>tone of voice</u> to help get their point across (see p.3).

2) Informal speech contains <u>non-fluency features</u> (things that interrupt the flow of speech) like <u>self-correction</u>, <u>pauses</u>, <u>repetition</u>, <u>fillers</u> ('sort of', 'I mean') and <u>false starts</u> (see p.4).

3) Speech also contains <u>phatic</u> (small talk) <u>expressions</u> like '<u>hello</u>' and '<u>how's things?</u>'. These are just a <u>friendly</u> way of greeting people — their <u>meaning isn't</u> particularly <u>important</u>.

Multi-Modal Talk contains Features of Speech AND Writing

Lots of texts are a <u>mixture</u> of <u>spoken</u> and <u>written</u> modes, especially electronic texts like <u>emails</u> and <u>text messages</u>.

1) Multi-modal texts are <u>written modes</u> that contain elements of <u>spoken language</u> — e.g. <u>phatic expressions</u> like '<u>hi</u>' and '<u>bye</u>'. They work like <u>written down</u> versions of <u>spoken</u> conversation.

2) <u>Text messages</u> need to be brief, so they tend to contain things like <u>phonetic spelling</u>, <u>clipping</u> and <u>initialisms</u> (see p.35).

3) <u>Instant messaging</u> is er... instant, so messages are typed very quickly and tend to contain lots of the same features as text messages.

4) Very <u>informal emails</u> between friends might contain lots of <u>text speak</u> too.

5) <u>Formal emails</u> are <u>less formal</u> than letters — e.g. they don't usually use <u>conventions</u> like writing the sender's address at the top. Paragraphs and sentences tend to be <u>shorter</u> too.

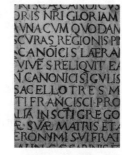

After years of study, experts finally realised that the inscription wasn't in Latin, it was in text speak.

Multi-modal? I prefer America's Next Top Modal...

It seems like a lot to take in, but a lot of this stuff you'll know all about from experience anyway — it's just a case of learning some fancy terms for things you do every day.

Worked Example and Practice Questions

Since you ask so nicely, I'm going to give you an example of an <u>informal email</u> between friends. And because I like you, I'll even point out some of the <u>features</u> from the previous page. Once you've had a good look at that, have a go at the <u>questions</u> to make sure you've taken everything in.

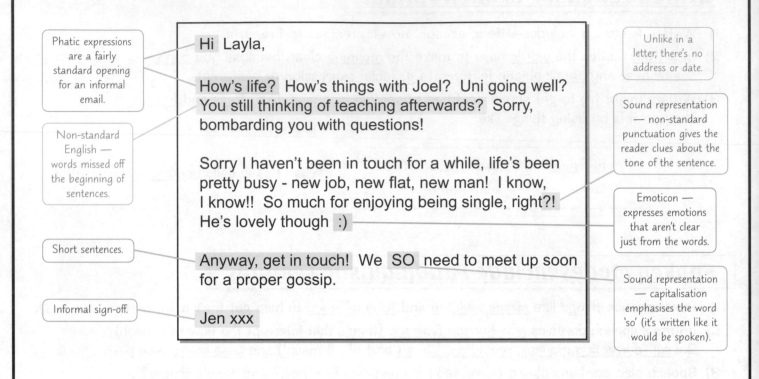

Phatic expressions are a fairly standard opening for an informal email.

Non-standard English — words missed off the beginning of sentences.

Short sentences.

Informal sign-off.

Hi Layla,

How's life? How's things with Joel? Uni going well? You still thinking of teaching afterwards? Sorry, bombarding you with questions!

Sorry I haven't been in touch for a while, life's been pretty busy - new job, new flat, new man! I know, I know!! So much for enjoying being single, right?! He's lovely though :)

Anyway, get in touch! We SO need to meet up soon for a proper gossip.

Jen xxx

Unlike in a letter, there's no address or date.

Sound representation — non-standard punctuation gives the reader clues about the tone of the sentence.

Emoticon — expresses emotions that aren't clear just from the words.

Sound representation — capitalisation emphasises the word 'so' (it's written like it would be spoken).

Q1 Give three examples of language that is in the written mode.

Q2 State two ways in which spoken language features can be shown in writing.

Q3 What is multi-modal talk?

Q4 Give two examples of texts that might contain multi-modal talk.

Texting

Beep-beep. Beep-beep...

Text Messages are Multi-Modal

1) Text messages contain features of written language — that's fairly obvious.

2) They also contain features of spoken language — things like saying 'hello' and 'goodbye' (phatic expressions), or using emoticons (like facial expressions) to get your meaning across.

3) Not all texts are the same. The purpose and audience affect the type of language used, so texting has its own sociolect, e.g. a text from your network provider would be more formal than one from a friend.

Text Speak is Non-Standard

1) Text speak is a compressed language — letters are often missed out or replaced with numbers or symbols. It developed because it was quicker and cheaper than typing words out in full on a phone keypad.

2) It's a non-standard form of the language, so it doesn't follow the same rules as some other types of written language.

3) It does still have some rules though — e.g. you normally miss out vowels not consonants.

No matter how many times it was explained to him, Brian never really got the hang of texting.

4) People have their own styles of texting. Some people shorten every word and don't use spaces, while others write quite formally. Most people are quite inconsistent, but text speak still has some common features:

FEATURE	EXAMPLE
Numbers and symbols instead of words	4 (for), & (and)
Clipping (shortened words), missing out vowels	jan (January), wk (week)
Phonetic spelling (words written how they sound)	c u (see you)
Acronyms* (just writing the first letter of each word)	rofl (Rolling On Floor Laughing)
Initialisms* (just writing the first letter of each word)	brb (Be Right Back)
Smileys / emoticons	;-) (wink)
Words missed out and simple sentences	be back soon
Non-standard grammar, punctuation and no capitals	im not bad hows u

*Watch out — it's easy to get confused between acronyms and initialisms. For acronyms the whole new word can be pronounced (e.g. ASBO) but for initialisms each letter is said separately (e.g. DNA).

Let's talk about texts, baby...

Texting might be a piece of cake for you young whippersnappers, but not everyone finds it so easy. My poor old mum doesn't know how to do punctuation, so she sends me texts like this — 'hello darling comma how are you question mark'. And my dad's fingers are too big for the buttons. Bless.

Texting

Text <u>messages</u> are a <u>fast</u> and <u>casual</u> form of communication. People like them because you can send one <u>quickly</u>, and <u>reply</u> to one whenever you want to (or just pretend you didn't get it...).

Text Language *has its own* Etiquette

There are certain <u>rules</u> you follow if you're talking to someone (this is <u>pragmatics</u> — see p.3). It's the same with texting, for example:

1) Writing a message entirely in <u>capitals</u> makes it look like you're <u>shouting</u>, so people do it for effect — e.g. 'WOOHOO'. This is <u>sound representation</u> (see p.33).

2) It's tricky to get across the <u>tone</u> you want in such a small space, so texts are open to <u>misinterpretation</u>. It's quite easy to <u>offend people</u> unintentionally, so you might put something like a winking face to show you're only joking.

3) Texts are <u>casual</u> and <u>quick</u>, so they lose <u>meaning</u> and <u>depth</u> — this means it's usually not seen as appropriate to use texts in <u>serious</u> or <u>formal</u> situations (e.g. dumping your girlfriend or quitting your job).

Text Speak *is Changing over Time*

1) Back in the day, mobiles <u>couldn't</u> do <u>predictive text</u>, and sending texts was more <u>expensive</u> than it is now. So text speak evolved to <u>save time</u> and <u>money</u>.

2) Now phones have got predictive text, it's often <u>quicker</u> and <u>easier</u> to type words out <u>in full</u>. This means that old-style text speak might be used <u>less</u> than it was a few years ago.

3) Text messages are used for thing like <u>advertising</u> and <u>TV voting</u>. <u>Standard spelling</u> and <u>punctuation</u> tend to be used for these purposes, so text speak might become more <u>conventional</u> over time.

4) Words also go in and out of <u>fashion</u> really quickly — e.g. <u>LOL</u> used to stand for '<u>lots of love</u>', but most people these days use it to mean '<u>laugh out loud</u>'.

Some people think Text Speak *is 'Bad' English*

1) Because text speak uses <u>non-standard English</u>, some people think it's '<u>incorrect</u>', hard to <u>understand</u> and means people will stop being able to <u>spell</u> words properly.

2) Other people say that text speak is <u>useful</u> and <u>appropriate</u> for text messages, but that it <u>shouldn't</u> be used in other contexts.

3) You could also argue that language always <u>changes</u>, and that spoken and written English have always contained <u>abbreviations</u> and <u>acronyms</u>. This means that text speak can be seen as just a <u>natural progression</u>.

2 txt or nt 2 txt... thts the qstn

Some people think that texting will lead to a generation of people who can't spell. But who decided the 'correct' way to spell anyway... Oo I've come over all anti-establishment. Time for a lie down.

Texting — Worked Example

I've got <u>loads of friends</u>, so I get hundreds of text messages a day. Here's an example of the kind of hilarious things we say to each other, with some <u>notes</u> on the <u>important features</u> of the <u>language</u>.

Non-standard English — no capital letters at the beginning of sentences.

Inconsistency — some words written out in full.

Acronym — 'lol' for 'laugh out loud'.

Compression — vowels missed out.

Non-standard punctuation — no apostrophe in 'he's'.

Sound representation — non-standard spelling used for emphasis. This shows that people don't always miss out letters in texts.

Ellipsis— '1.30 is fine'.

Phonetic spelling of 'love'.

Phonetic spelling of 'would be good'.

You don't usually sign your name at the end of the text, because it's normally saved in the other person's phone. This makes it different from a letter.

People often write the wrong word if they're using predictive text. This should say 'me'.

Emoticon — used to make feelings clear.

Clipping — 'Saturday afternoon'.

Non-standard English — number instead of letter.

Kisses / hugs are a feature of informal written language. They're also part of this person's individual texting style.

Symbol instead of letter.

A

hey hows it goin gona be in ldn this wknd if ur around? wud b gud 2 catch up etc - cud mayb hav lunch... xox

B

Hey, am good thanks, how about you? How are things with the new boyf? Heard you'd been on the prowl lol. Yeh lunch would be good, but give me dates give of times!!

A

ok ok! sat or sun, either gud for me so wheneva ur free. gr8with james thnx-hes really sweet :) whos bin sayin iv bin on the prowl tho?!xox

B

I never reveal my sources lol. coooool ok how about sat aft? Don't mind what time

A

1.30? wot dya fancy 4 munch xox

B

Yep 1.30 fine. How am i sposed to know what i'm gona want to eat now?! Let's just meet up somewhere and decide yeh?

A

soz luv!! alrite station @half 1?xox

Texting — Practice Questions

Sending texts may be simple, but it's not allowed in the controlled assessment... Instead, you have to know how to <u>write about</u> them, so have a go at these <u>questions</u> to check you're on track.

Q1   Why did text speak develop? Choose one answer.

    a) because schools stopped teaching grammar

    b) because society is becoming less formal

    c) because it was easier and cheaper to type shorter versions of words on mobiles

Q2   What does 'compression' mean in terms of text speak?

Q3   Is text speak a standard form of the language?

Q4   What is an acronym?

Q5   Describe the examples of non-standard English in these sentences.
(Hint — there might be more than one thing per sentence.)

a) u coming later	c) no way m8	e) il come soon
b) @ my mums	d) shes like my bff	f) out wiv greg

Q6   Write out this text using phonetic spelling:

Are you too busy to see me later?

Q7   What concerns do some people have about text speak?

Texting — Practice Example

More texts from another one of my <u>many friends</u>... Have a <u>read through</u> them and answer the <u>questions</u>. Use the information on pages 35-36 to help you <u>analyse</u> the <u>language</u>.

A

k so not bothered 2 book anything
coz cant really think but how bout just
seeing whats on at the cinema :)

1) What's this?

2) What's the proper term for when words are written like this?

B

haha no probs.dunno about pictures im
a bit skint at the mo

A

can get 241 if we go b4 7

3) What's going on here?

4) What could you say about the punctuation here?

B

oh yeh forgot about that-lets do it!

A

cool :) wot time u wana meet

5) What word is missing here?

B

hmm well i want a lie in so say 5?

6) Is this a feature of written language or spoken language?

A

5 4 a lie in,as in 5pm?LAZY :-p

7) Why do you think there aren't any spaces after the punctuation?

B

k 4 then...

A

yeh cool, 4 at the cinema? :)

8) What's going on here?

B

yup c u there. will try not to be l8 ;) x

9) What's this?

10) Is this a feature of written language or spoken language?

A

blve that wen i c it lol. cu later

11) Write a mini-essay where you analyse the language features in this extract.
You don't just have to focus on the features that have been highlighted in the blue boxes.

Online Talk

The internet has changed the way that people <u>communicate</u> and the kind of <u>language</u> that they use. Some of the best examples of this are <u>emails</u>, <u>instant messaging</u>, <u>blogs</u> and <u>chat rooms</u>.

Online Talk is Multi-Modal

1) <u>Online talk</u> is <u>written</u> language that contains elements of <u>spoken</u> language.

2) It often contains lots of <u>netspeak</u> (like <u>text speak</u>, but on the internet), e.g. <u>clipping</u> and <u>acronyms</u>.

3) How <u>formal</u> the language is depends on its <u>form</u> (e.g. email, chatroom posting), <u>audience</u> (friend, colleague, grandma) and <u>purpose</u> (arranging a meeting, catching up, sharing info).

4) The more <u>spoken</u> language features it contains, the <u>less formal</u> it is.

Before the internet was invented, people had to make their own entertainment.

Emails can be Formal or Informal

<u>Emails</u> are usually typed on a full-sized keyboard, and they have <u>no word limit</u>, so they don't have to be as <u>brief</u> as <u>text messages</u>.

1) <u>Emails</u> with a <u>formal purpose</u> (e.g. between businesses) tend to use <u>Standard English</u>.

2) This is to make sure that the writer is <u>taken seriously</u>, and also so that everyone can <u>understand</u> the language.

3) However, even quite <u>formal emails</u> are still <u>multi-modal</u>. This is because they often contain <u>spoken language features</u>, e.g. <u>phatic</u> expressions like 'hi' and 'see you'.

4) <u>Informal emails</u> (e.g. between friends and family) might contain time-saving devices like <u>clipping</u>, <u>missing punctuation</u> or any of the features of <u>text speak</u> (see p.35).

Emails can be Instant

1) You can reply to an email pretty much <u>immediately</u>. This makes them a lot more like <u>spontaneous conversation</u> than a traditional letter.

2) It means that the <u>language</u> used in them is often quite <u>direct</u>, and things like <u>context</u> aren't always explained. For example:

> Hi Claire,
>
> What time are we meeting today? I've forgotten...
>
> Thanks
>
> Polly

Virtual men — e-males...

Ho hum, it's all getting a bit simple now really. If this stuff about emails is too easy, or you're just into punishment, try putting the page next to a mirror and reading it all backwards or something.

Online Talk

So we've done <u>emails</u> — they were dead easy. Now it's <u>instant message</u> time.

Instant Messages <u>are</u> Informal

1) <u>Instant messages</u> tend to contain more <u>spoken language</u> and <u>netspeak</u> features than emails.

2) Again, there are <u>no set conventions</u>, so people often use <u>non-standard English</u>.

3) People are online <u>at the same time</u>, so 'chats' are <u>spontaneous</u>, and you <u>expect interaction</u> pretty much <u>straight away</u>.

4) This means that people type very quickly, so it's handy to use <u>netspeak</u> features like <u>clipping</u> and <u>acronyms</u>.

5) The language might reflect the speaker's <u>idiolect</u> (e.g. using 'yup' or 'yeah' instead of 'yes', saying 'ah' instead of 'I', and using <u>dialect</u> words).

6) You can also look out for how different <u>sociolects</u> are used in different <u>contexts</u> (p.14-15), e.g. people might use less netspeak if they're chatting to their <u>mum</u> than to their <u>friends</u>.

People often use <u>Sound Representation</u>

1) <u>Paralinguistic features</u> like tone of voice are shown by using <u>sound representation</u>, e.g. <u>capitalisation</u> or <u>non-standard spelling/punctuation</u>.

2) For example, you might write 'NOOOOOO waaaaaaaaay!?!' to make it clear that if you were speaking out loud you'd be shouting, and would sound really surprised (although people do tend to exaggerate more when they write things like this down).

3) <u>Emoticons</u> can help get across how serious you are. There are loads of these to choose from when you're instant messaging — e.g. ones that dance around, wink, explode, give you bunches of flowers etc etc...

You usually <u>Take Turns</u> when you're Messaging

People often show whose <u>turn</u> it is by asking a <u>question</u> at the <u>end</u> of each message, for example:

Jim:	How u doin?
Saz:	gud thnx, u
Jim:	yeh not bad,you out later?

Ed: u typin wiv ur feet again?
Hayley: yeh it rox!! u never tried it?
Ed: nah. hands 4 me evry time
Hayley: lol

Keeping someone <u>waiting</u> for a long time before you reply could be seen as <u>rude</u>, so people use <u>initialisms</u> like 'BRB' ('be right back') or 'GTG' ('got to go') to show that they'll be out of touch for a while.

Learn all this and you'll be ROFLing...

Call me a miserable old git, but I can't remember a single time when I've found something so amusing that I've actually rolled on the floor laughing. Although I did once burst with laughter.

Online Talk

Personally I'm not keen on the word <u>blog</u>. It kind of reminds me of throwing up. Still, you don't have to like it, you just have to read it. And maybe it doesn't even remind you of sick anyway, who knows...

Blogs are like Public Diaries

1) <u>Weblogs</u> (<u>blogs</u> for short) let people share their thoughts and opinions with the rest of the world.

2) <u>Bloggers</u> don't necessarily expect to <u>interact</u> with the people reading their blog. Some readers might <u>post</u> things on the website, but the interaction <u>isn't instant</u> like it is with instant messaging.

3) Blogs are usually <u>unregulated</u> and <u>uncensored</u>, and there are <u>no language conventions</u>. This means that the language is <u>controlled entirely by the writer</u>.

4) Some blogs (e.g. politicians' blogs) are written in <u>Standard English</u>, which makes them more <u>accessible</u> for a <u>wider audience</u> and makes them seem more <u>professional</u>.

5) Other blog writers use the same kinds of <u>spoken language features</u> that they'd use in <u>text messages</u>.

- <u>Social networking sites</u> like Facebook and Twitter act like <u>microblogs</u> — people record what they're doing during the day. They're used by a <u>range</u> of people, so there's <u>huge variety</u> in the <u>language</u> used.
- People might use popular <u>sociolects</u> to show that they're part of the '<u>in crowd</u>'.
- Some bloggers also <u>exaggerate</u> their <u>idiolect</u> in what they type. This helps people get more of an idea of their <u>background</u> and <u>personality</u>.

Different Types of Websites use Different Language

1) <u>Chat rooms</u> and <u>forums</u> are a bit like <u>instant messaging</u>, but instead of talking to one person or just a few friends, you're talking to <u>everyone</u> else who's on the same site.

2) Forums are often based on <u>hobbies</u> or <u>interests</u>, so they contain subject-specific <u>jargon</u>.

3) Chat room conversations tend to be <u>quick</u>, so <u>netspeak</u> is often used to save time.

The Internet has had a big Impact on English

- The internet has changed the English language in lots of ways — e.g. there are lots of <u>new words</u> about it, like 'website', 'netiquette' and 'search engine'.
- People all over the world are now <u>connected</u>, so it's easier for <u>different languages</u> and <u>sociolects</u> to <u>blend</u> and change faster then they ever have before.
- It's also changing the way that people <u>speak</u>. Some people now use features of online talk in speech, e.g. they might say 'lol' in a spoken conversation. This is particularly true of <u>young people</u>, and shows how <u>technology</u> is <u>changing</u> the language.

Check out my blog — 1412 entries about my cats...

...and 1246 entries about my lack of a boyfriend. I just don't understand it, I mean, I'm interesting and funny, plus I've got a huge collection of stuffed toys. Any man would be lucky to have me.

Online Talk — Worked Example

You need to be able to recognise different <u>features</u> of online talk when you see them. Here's an <u>example</u> of an instant messenger conversation that I've helpfully marked up for you.

Non-standard English — no capital letters at the beginning of sentences.

Sound representation — phonetic spelling of a spoken language feature.

Sound representation — non-standard punctuation to show the tone of the sentence.

Sound representation — non-standard spelling to emphasise the word.

Informal abbreviation of 'sorry' saves time.

Initialism — 'OMG' for 'Oh My God'.

Non-standard English — number instead of word.

Ellipsis — the word 'I'll' has been missed out here.

Emoticon.

Non-standard English — symbol instead of 'at'.

Inconsistent spelling of the same word.

Initialism — 'ttyl' for 'talk to you later'.

Misinterpretation — A hasn't replied, so B wonders if they've gone.

Phonetic spelling of some words.

Non-standard punctuation — no apostrophe in 'she's'.

Slurring together of words (elision) is a feature of spoken language.

A: hey sweetie, hows u?

B: gud thanx, u?

A: ok. am @ emmas doin history coursework ☹

B: ugh havent started mine. u & em r sooooo lucky u got put togeva, i got put wiv freaky ian

A: lol. least hes brainy, u'll get an A for sure ☺

B: yeahhh but... i wanna be wiv u guys!!!

A: i no!!! sooooo wish we cud all do it togevr. oooh, hannah's just come on - ttyl

B: ok.

B: u there?

A: soz hun, jus seein if han's ok. u no she split wiv Harry?

B: OMG. wen?

A: afta skool 2day. he dumped her in front of evry1...

B: OMG. poor han. is she ok?

A: not gr8. shes comin ova now. u wanna cum ova 2?

B: be ther in 20. ill bring chocolate

Online Talk — Worked Example

So, spending time on Facebook now counts as homework too. Tcchhh, it wasn't like that in my day. Tear yourself away from your computer and have a squizz at this thread from a rock climbing forum.

Phatic expressions make the request sound friendly and polite.

A: hey guys. me & the missus r off to the Dales nxt wknd. any tips for good (non-tourist!) climbs?

Sound representation — capitals and non-standard punctuation.

B: Nice one m8, dales are awsum! Try Gilberts Edge nr brantmoor — QUALITY!!!

Climbing-specific jargon.

A: cheers mate forgot to say we're both about a grade 5

Non-standard English — no capital letters or punctuation.

C: Gilbert's Edge is a great route. It gets pretty busy though... My top tip — Willet Tor, near Fenstone.

Variation in style — C uses Standard English, D uses lots of netspeak.

D: Dales!! ace!! me & mine used to cruz rnd lookin 4 gud boulderin spots. bst we found was glassley heights — jsut off the B648 nr stoke worthy

Typing quickly means that typos are common.

Regional dialect word.

A: great, ta guys. should give us summat to work with :o)

Emoticon — used here to show happiness and enthusiasm.

E: hey hey. soz to crash this thread lol. just wondrd if ne1 cud recommend sum gud shoes — thinkin of gettin the new Rockgod Scramblers — ne1 tried em?

Inconsistency — some words written out in full.

C: No worries. A friend of mine just got a pair and swears by them. They're on offer at the mo at SportsWorld — I've got a discount code if you're interested.

Clipping.

Misinterpretation — E assumes that C is male.

E: nice 1 m8 ur a proper gent

Sound representation — non-standard punctuation indicates pauses.

C: Er... thank you... I'm actually a laydeee, but the light's quite dim in here ;)

Sound representation — non-standard spelling to show that the tone is light and humorous.

Sound representation — phonetic spelling of a spoken language feature.

E: oh heck, soz luv. im sure ur gorgeous ;) lol

Acronym.

C: Thank you, I am.

Online Talk — Practice Questions

Nobody panic, I haven't forgotten the <u>practice questions</u>, I just got a bit carried away with examples. Here they are, knock yourself out. I'm off for a little lie down to get over all the excitement.

Q1   Give an example of a phatic expression that might be used in an email.

Q2   How would the language of a business email be different from the language used in an instant message to a friend?

Q3   Why is netspeak often used in instant messages?

Q4   Explain how paralinguistic features can be shown in online talk.

Q5   How do people take turns when they're talking online?

Q6   What do people use blogs for?

Q7   Give one example of how the internet has changed English.

Online Talk — Practice Example

Pssst, yeah you, over here... I've got a lovely <u>example</u> of an <u>instant messenger</u> conversation here. It's going cheap. Look, I tell you what, because I like the look of you I'm going to let you have it for nothing. Just don't tell anyone, or my rep will be in tatters...

1) What's this?

A: alrite m8, wot u doin?

2) What's it called when letters are missed out like this?

B: Revisin. Got me drivin test 2moz am. Told ya lst wk

3) Is this a feature of written language or spoken language?

A: Oops my bad. Gd luk. u scared?

B: Kinda. had 2 lsns 2 day. Only hit kerb once ;o)

4) What's the proper term for when words are slurred together like this?

A: ur dangerous man - aint never gonna get in the car wiv you lol

6) What could you say about the punctuation here?

B: Oh yeah. Once I got wheels yule be beggin

A: Y wd I wanna commit suicide? Im 2 young 2 die :)

B: NEway don't worry I aint gonna pass.

5) What's this? Why is it used here?

A: That's gud man. Think how many lives ur savin.

7) What's this?

B: LMAO... not. Wot u up to 2nite?

8) Why does the person end with a question?

9) What's going on here?

A: dunno. mebbe playin some video games wiv Tariq. u fancy it?

B: Nah, off out to practise wiv me mum...

A: lol well gis a call wen ur dun n we'll celebr8 ;)

10) What's going on here?

11) Write a mini-essay where you analyse the language features in this extract. You don't just have to focus on the features that have been highlighted in the blue boxes.

Online Talk — Practice Example

Well, this is it. Your last <u>practice example</u>. I know it's terribly sad, but don't worry, all the unused practice examples have been sent off to a big factory to get recycled into plastic bags. Apart from the bad ones. They're going to be made into scratching posts for cows. Anyway, this blog is one of the lucky ones that made the cut. Read and enjoy.

1) Why has the writer chosen to use Standard English?

2) What's this?

One man's crusade against linguistic laxity
by Gerald Pearson

As my regular readers will know, I'm fighting an ongoing battle to prevent the tragic decline of language skills in today's youth. This week heralds a new personal nadir; on Monday I saw Gideon 'instant messaging' a friend the following tripe: 'OMG - aged p jus trpd ova my sktbrd & i got it on flm. utube gold. ROFLMAO!!!' To think my own son is capable of such banality! I'm unable to interpret what on earth he's talking about, but naturally I withdrew his internet rights immediately. I've told him he cna have them back once he's finished reading War and Peace.

3) What's going on here?

4) What's going on here?

I can only be grateful that we removed Felicity to finishing school in Switzerland after the text messaging fiasco. At least she's out of temptation's way.

My crusade hit another stumbling block this week, when Gideon's blasted school (excuse my imprecation, but it really is most aggravating) finally replied to my letter (see my entry for the 12th March). Not only did they assert that they 'do not have the authority or inclination' to ban the use of mobile phones outside of school hours, they also informed me that 'text speak' is to be added to the syllabus as part of the English Language GCSE!?! A dreadful setback, dear readers, there's no doubt of that, but I shall not yield!

5) Why has the writer put these words in inverted commas?

6) What can you say about the punctuation here?

7) What's this?

Ah, dearest wife is calling, I must away. Goodbye all.

8) What's this?

9) Write a mini-essay where you analyse the language features in this extract. You don't just have to focus on the features that have been highlighted in the blue boxes.

What You Have to Do

For <u>Unit 3</u> <u>Part C</u> (Spoken Language Study) you have to do a <u>Controlled Assessment Task</u>. This is worth <u>10%</u> of the total mark for your GCSE. It doesn't sound like much but it's marks in the bag.

You get to Choose the Aspects of Spoken Language you like

1) You have to choose <u>one task</u> out of a choice of <u>six</u>.

2) There are <u>two tasks</u> for each of the following categories:

- Social attitudes to spoken language (e.g. people's attitudes to slang)
- Spoken genres (e.g. soap scripts, radio adverts, speeches)
- Multi-modal talk (e.g. text messaging, online chat)

3) You write your answer under <u>supervised conditions</u>. You'll have up to <u>three hours</u> to write <u>800-1000 words</u>, and the time might be <u>spread over</u> two or more sessions.

These are the Kinds of Topic you will be Asked to Explore

Remember you only have to do <u>one task</u> out of the six. You might have to discuss things like:

1) Your <u>own language</u> (idiolect) and attitudes of others to it.
2) The features of the speech used in a <u>particular occupation</u> (such as nursing).
3) The language of a spoken genre, e.g. radio adverts.
4) Features of <u>public talk</u> (such as a political speech).
5) How <u>interaction</u> takes place in <u>electronic communication</u> (e.g. chatrooms).
6) The language of <u>text messaging</u> (e.g. how it's abbreviated).

You can Prepare for your Controlled Assessment

1) You can <u>work in small groups</u> and get help from your <u>teacher</u> when you're <u>planning your answer</u>.

2) You can take <u>brief notes from your plan</u> into the assessment with you, but <u>NOT drafts</u>.

3) Any work you do during the <u>supervised sessions</u> needs to be <u>handed in</u> at the end to your teacher. You'll <u>get it back</u> at the start of the next session.

4) This preparation time <u>doesn't</u> count as part of the 2-3 hours for writing up your work.

You're Allowed to use Computers to Collect Your Data

1) You can use the <u>internet</u> if you need to during these supervised sessions to collect data (for example, a soap opera script, a video clip, an extract from some online chat).

2) You <u>won't</u> be allowed to use it in the <u>final write-up</u> though.

3) Your final piece can be <u>handwritten</u> or <u>written on the computer</u>.

A cordless melon's tents* — not so scary from that angle...

Not the most fascinating page, I'm sure you'll agree, but it helps to know exactly what you're going to have to do, and how long you're going to have to do it, and how many words you're going to...

*Yes, that is an anagram of 'controlled assessment'.

How to Collect Data

Your teacher might give you some <u>data</u> to <u>analyse</u>, or tell you <u>where</u> to get it from. But if you're super-keen and want to <u>collect your own</u>, this page tells you how.

You can get lots of Different Kinds of Data

There are all sorts of different <u>types</u> of data that you could look at for your controlled assessment:

1) <u>Transcripts</u> of <u>real dialogue</u> that you've recorded — e.g. your friends chatting.
2) <u>Transcripts</u> of <u>audio</u> or audio-visual clips — e.g. a transcript of a radio or TV interview.
3) <u>Text messages</u> or <u>online chat</u> conversations.
4) <u>Scripted language</u>, such as a radio advert, or a TV news broadcast, or a public speech.
5) Newspaper <u>articles</u>, or other material that shows <u>attitudes</u> to <u>spoken</u> language.
6) There's also data you can use on the <u>internet</u>, or you might want to record parts of a <u>radio</u> or <u>TV</u> programme.

Remember, the preparation time is for collecting your data or making a transcript, and planning your answer. It doesn't count towards the 2-3 hours' writing time.

You might want to Record People Talking

1) <u>Transcripts</u> of people talking can be great for looking at spoken language — they can show you features like <u>dialect</u>, <u>sociolect</u>, <u>idiolect</u>, <u>slang</u> etc.
2) You could <u>make your own</u>, or your teacher might give you one to study.
3) To get a transcript, you have to make a <u>recording</u> of some people talking first.
4) Whoever you record, you should get their <u>permission</u> to use what they say.
5) Make sure that what you record <u>isn't</u> too <u>short</u>, otherwise you might not have <u>enough data</u> to comment on. It's better to let the recording roll on and get too much at first.
6) When you play it back, <u>choose</u> a part of it that you think has the most <u>potential</u> for <u>investigation</u>.

Writing a Transcript is Hard Work

1) For a transcript, your aim is to capture <u>exactly</u> what's been said.
2) Write down all the <u>words</u>, as well as the <u>pauses</u> and the <u>fillers</u> (like 'er' and 'erm'). You should also transcribe any <u>overlaps</u>, <u>false starts</u> and <u>repetitions</u>.
3) This means you'll have to <u>stop and start</u> the track you've recorded <u>little by little</u> to give you time to <u>write it down</u>.

As a rough guide — transcribing a minute of recorded conversation takes about 15 minutes, so don't give yourself too much to do.

Data? — nah, I'd rather just be good friends with her...

Getting hold of some top-notch data is really worthwhile. It's worth taking the time to record and write a transcript — there's nothing worse than trying to say something useful about lousy data.

How to Analyse Data

Once you've got your data, it's <u>showtime</u>...
(By that I mean time for you to start analysing it.)

Write Down the Basic Information first

Make sure you <u>jot down</u> the really <u>obvious</u> things that you'll be considering in your analysis.

1) The first thing to do is to identify what <u>kind</u> of <u>spoken language</u> it is. Write down whether it's a <u>dialogue</u>, a <u>speech</u> or a radio <u>advert</u>, for example.

2) Write down what you know about the speakers — e.g. their <u>age</u>, <u>gender</u>, <u>job</u> and <u>social</u> and <u>regional</u> background.

3) Identify the <u>topic</u> too. For example, if it's two musicians talking, there will be particular musical <u>jargon</u> words to look out for.

4) Look at the <u>context</u> — e.g. if it's a transcript of a <u>job interview</u>, you might expect it to contain formal speech and <u>occupational sociolect</u>.

Get Stuck In and Start Analysing the Actual Language

1) Look out for <u>non-fluency</u> features such as <u>pauses</u>, <u>hesitations</u>, <u>fillers</u>, <u>false starts</u>, <u>repetition</u>.

2) Listen out for <u>accents</u> and features such as <u>tone of voice</u> and <u>volume</u>.

3) You might find elements of non-standard <u>grammar</u> (e.g. 'We was trying our hardest') to mention.

4) The way the speakers <u>interact</u> is important too — e.g. who speaks most and what they call each other.

5) If you're looking at text, email and chat language, you may need to comment on how <u>visual symbols</u>, like <u>emoticons</u>, are used to represent features of spoken language.

Have a look at the <u>example data</u> and <u>analysis</u> below for an idea of the sort of stuff to include:

Data:

A: Where r u? :-s
B: town
A: Town? Sposd 2 b HERE! its 7 already.
B: Oh yeah. soz. Fort we was meetin at 8.
A: c u soon.
B: OK :-)

What you could write:

This is a text 'conversation' between two people talking about arrangements to meet up.

You can tell the people know each other because there is no phatic language — instead person A begins with a direct question. The conversation has a conventional pattern that you might expect in spoken dialogue. It starts with a question, followed by turn-taking and a closing comment.

It's harder to tell in a text conversation who is in control of the conversation, and how people are feeling, because there aren't any paralinguistic features. To get over this problem, person A uses word representation to suggest that they are shouting and irritated — 'HERE'. They then put an exclamation mark to show that they aren't really serious. Both people also use smileys to suggest their facial expressions. The conversation contains other typical features of text language — e.g. phonetic spelling ('Fort' for 'Thought') which may reflect the informal tone intended or the need to save time or space. This shows the sociolect of the speakers, and forms part of their identity.

28 Days' Data — now that would be scary...

It's really helpful to think about the speakers and the topic they're discussing before you start analysing the language. That way you can think about which linguistic features to look out for.

How to Write Up the Controlled Assessment

The sample analysis at the bottom of the previous page was just a little taster of what you should be aiming to write in your controlled assessment. This page'll tell you how to write a really great analysis.

Think about How you'll Structure your Work

1) You need to make sure that what you write has a clear structure.
2) A three-part structure is the best: introduction, data analysis, evaluation.
3) When you give in your final draft, make sure you also hand in all your data and any preliminary notes you've made.

Make Sure you have a Strong Introduction

1) In your introduction you need to say what kind of spoken language you're looking at, how you collected it, and what features of it you are going to investigate and discuss.
2) Say something about the context of your data. For example, 'this is an informal radio interview taken from a Radio 1 broadcast, aimed at young people'.

The Data Analysis should be the Main Bit of your Answer

1) This will be the longest and most important part of your investigation.
2) You need to take a methodical approach, making sure that each paragraph has a particular focus.
3) For example, you could plan to write paragraphs which each focus on one of these features:

- Vocabulary (e.g. slang, jargon, dialect words, occupational sociolect)
- Sounds (e.g. accent/dialect features such as dropping consonants)
- Grammar (e.g. standard or non-standard)
- Non-fluency features (e.g. pauses, false starts, overlapping)
- Paralinguistic features (e.g. loudness, stress, pitch)
- Pragmatics (e.g. turn-taking, politeness words, implied meanings)
- Attitudes towards language (e.g. 'jargon is good', 'jargon is bad')

4) How much you write about each of these will depend on your data. For example, you might find that there's not much to write about grammar but plenty to write about vocabulary or sounds.

Finish with a Broad Evaluation

1) In your final paragraph, you should sum up your findings, drawing all your ideas together.
2) Write about the bits that you found difficult as well as the bits you thought you did well.
3) Remember to think critically about your data. For example, maybe the speakers weren't speaking naturally because they knew they were being recorded (this is called the observer's paradox).

Blah blah pun — something something joke...

You get the idea. If you can get a good structure from the start, your answer should fall effortlessly into place. The controlled assessment can be a gold mine of marks if you plan properly.

Sample Task — Social Attitudes to Spoken Language

There will be two tasks to choose from on social attitudes to spoken language.

Here's an Example of what you can Expect...

You could choose a task for your controlled assessment that looks a bit like the one below.

> Reflect on the speech used by young people.
> What attitudes to this language are you aware of from others?

1) You might want to collect your own data for this, but your teacher could choose it for you.

2) To get the data you could ask some young people you know such as friends or classmates to let you record them talking.

3) It might be a good idea to collect some data about attitudes to spoken language — e.g. a newspaper article about teenage slang.

...and Here's what your Data might look like

You'll probably want to analyse a slightly longer transcript than the one we've done here.

Aimee:	why don't we go to Roxy's (.) yeah Roxy's (1) last week was awesome
Mo:	yeah (.) Roxy's is good but (.) er it's so expensive babe (.) anyways (1) erm don't get paid till Saturday
Aimee:	the DJ was sick though Mo (.) er can't you borrow some dosh from Akkie
Mo:	nah (.) you know what he's like (.) mean or what
Aimee:	// well I could lend you some
Mo:	nah babe (1) I'm always (.) I've been cadgin off of you loads (.) it ain't fair
Aimee:	I could come round to yours then
Mo:	would you (.) hey but you don't get don't get to go out then so it's
Aimee:	// I'm not that bothered and erm (.) we can like watch a film or somethin (2) yeah an we could we could go to Dino's like get a pizza (.) or somethin
Mo:	// yeah but I'm payin babe
Aimee:	you just said you ain't got none
Mo:	I got some money (2) just just not enough to go to Roxy's
Aimee:	OK hun (.) that'll be cool

Key
(1) = pause in seconds
(.) = micropause

To give you an idea of what you could say about this data, there's a sample answer on page 53.

Hands up if reading that made you want a pizza too...

Make sure you've got a shed-load of data so you can pick an interesting section to discuss. Once you've got a recording and a transcript, get on the phone to Dino's and celebrate in style. Mmmm.

Sample Answer — Social Attitudes to Spoken Language

In your <u>write-up</u> you need to mention the <u>relevant things</u> you've spotted in your data and what they tell you about the spoken language you're studying. Here's a sample answer to give you some ideas.

Remember to Focus your answer on Social Attitudes

It's good to address the question in a clear introduction.

> Social attitudes towards the way young people speak are often quite negative. For example, some people think that teenagers use too much slang, and too many 'vague' words such as 'like' and 'sort of', which stop them from getting their point across clearly. People often argue that when teenagers use non-standard English they aren't using 'proper' English, and that this is ruining the language.

Good use of paragraphs — this one's specifically about slang and sociolect.

> The speakers in this extract are both in year 11. They use informal slang words that are used a lot in our school now — for example, changing the meaning of 'sick' to mean 'good'. This shows that the speakers are using a particular sociolect, that they might not use if they were in a different context, like speaking to a teacher. They use this sociolect to show that they are part of the 'in' crowd, and to exclude people who don't understand it.

Link the language feature to the context.

> You can see some features of regional dialect and accent in the transcript. For example, the word 'ain't' is a feature of Estuary English, which is the dialect both of them use. Mo uses it to mean 'isn't' when he says 'it ain't fair'. Aimee uses it to mean 'haven't' when she says 'you aint got none'. Mo also uses non-standard grammar when he says 'I've been cadgin off of you loads'. A feature of their pronunciation is that they both miss off consonants at the ends of words — for example 'cadgin', 'somethin'. This is part of their Estuary English accent, and it's common in casual speech, especially between young people. The speakers in this conversation may use Estuary English because it's used in the media and is seen as a trendy accent.

Good use of technical terms.

Always support your points with specific examples.

> The address terms they use show that the relationship between them is informal and affectionate. 'Babe' seems to be specific to Mo's idiolect, while 'hun' is part of Aimee's. Another feature of Aimee's idiolect is how she forms sentences. She uses the structure 'like... or somethin' twice — e.g. 'we can like watch a film or somethin'. You could argue that when teenagers use this kind of 'vague' language it shows that they can't get their point across clearly. However, Aimee is actually showing that she is just making a suggestion, and doesn't mind what they do.

Address opposite points of view to show that you're thinking about different social attitudes.

> The conversation contains non-fluency features like fillers ('er' and 'erm'), repetition ('just just') and false starts ('I'm always I've been cadgin off of you loads'). Some people might argue that this is a sign that the speakers can't speak clearly because they are teenagers. On the other hand, you could say that this is typical in most spontaneous conversations, because the speakers haven't planned what they are going to say.

> The speakers take turns, but there's a lot of overlap and interruption. This isn't usually a rude thing to do, for example Aimee interrupts Mo to say 'I'm not that bothered'. This is an example of pragmatics because by interrupting him, she is trying to reassure him that she doesn't mind whether they go out or not.

Good conclusion — links back to the task and your own data.

> In conclusion, my data helps to show that when teenagers are talking to each other in an informal context, their sociolect does contain slang and non-standard grammar. However, this doesn't mean that they are speaking incorrectly. It's appropriate for the informal context of the conversation, and it identifies them as part of a social group.

Sample Task — Spoken Genres

Just like for <u>social attitudes to spoken language</u>, you can <u>choose</u> from <u>two tasks</u> for <u>spoken genres</u>.

Here is an Example of what you can Expect...

Explore the language features of a type of talk in the media, such as a television or radio script.

1) Your teacher might give you an <u>extract</u> from some spoken language in the media to work with, or you might have to find your own.

2) To come up with your own, you can either <u>transcribe</u> one or find something on the <u>internet</u>.

3) Your extract is likely to be <u>longer</u> than the one below.

Not to be confused with 1981's Punk-Jazz sensations, 'Broken Genres'.

...and Here's what your Data might look like

Tim: [*blustering*] Now look here, Inspector, I don't know what the problem is here but you really can't go round accusing people like this. You have absolutely no evid-

McRae: [*interrupts sharply*] No evidence, Mr Montgomery? I think you'll find I have all the evidence I need to make sure you and your *sister* won't be seeing daylight for quite some time.

Tim: [*gasps involuntarily*] My-my sister? But I don't have a -

McRae: [*loudly and angrily*] Don't take me for a fool! Sergeant, bring in Miss Montgomery. [*Turns and looks hard at Tim*] Or *Miss Brown*, as she's been calling herself lately.

Tim: [*regaining his composure*] *Miss Brown*? [*He laughs*] My cleaning lady? Really, Inspector, I must say I credited you with a bit more intelligence than that. Why, the woman's common as muck. [*With disgust*] Certainly no relative of mine.

Enter Sergeant Reeves and Sally.

Sally: Why 'ello there, Inspector, was yer after another o' me home-made stotties?

McRae: You can drop the act, *Miss Montgomery*. You may as well come clean, I know you have the manuscript, and what's more I can prove it.

Sally: [*a little too quickly*] Manuscript, sir? I- I'm sure I don't know nothin' about no manuscript. [*Holds her hands up as if in defeat*] Why, I can't even read, me.

To give you an idea of what you could say about this data, there's a <u>sample answer</u> on page 55.

Don't stop now — it's just getting interesting...

Oh no, that's the end of the extract and I've got more questions than a three-hour maths exam — just who is Sally, where's the missing manuscript, and what on earth's a stottie...

Sample Answer — Spoken Genres

The <u>sample answer</u> on this page will hopefully give you an idea of the sort of <u>features</u> to <u>pick up on</u>.

Remember to Focus your answer on Spoken Genres

It's a good idea to state early on what it is that you're going to analyse.

Television and radio dramas engage the audience's attention, because they are scripted to sound like real-life speech, but in order to flow, they have to be easier to follow than spontaneous conversation. Script-writers can make scripted speech sound natural by using regional accents or dialects, slang, non-fluency features (e.g. fillers and interruption) and paralinguistic features like stress, tone and volume. I would expect to see examples of all of these elements in most scripts.

Give examples to support your points.

The first thing that stands out in this TV drama script is the use of non-standard English for the character of Sally. She uses non-standard grammar and pronunciation (e.g. a double negative in 'I don't know nothin'' and 'yer' instead of 'you') and dialect words (e.g. 'stotties'). These features show that the character would have a regional accent and dialect, which may be used to suggest certain things about this character. For example, a stronger accent and dialect might imply that she is less well educated than the other characters, and therefore she has less power than them.

When you're looking at a script, everything's been planned, so it's good to talk about why the writer used a particular technique.

There are some instances of non-fluency features in the script, although not as many as would be found in spontaneous conversation. On two occasions McRae interrupts Tim. These interruptions demonstrate that McRae holds the power in the conversation, and also imply that he is irritated with Tim, which gives the actor clues about how to play the character. The script-writer has made sure that the interruptions don't affect the audience's understanding of the dialogue — for example by having McRae finish Tim's sentence ("No evidence, Mr Montgomery?"). The other non-fluency features are repetition ("My-my sister?") and false starts ("I- I'm"), which I think are there to show that the characters are nervous. Pauses are shown by punctuation and stage directions. For example, the full stop and stage direction 'turns and looks hard at Tim', suggests that there's a long pause to build suspense before McRae reveals Tim's sister's identity.

Impressive technical term.

The stage directions help to show paralinguistic features. For example, 'loudly and angrily' shows the volume and tone of voice that the actor should use. The italics show which words should be stressed, e.g. 'your *sister*'. As well as how words sound, paralinguistic features include non-verbal communication like facial expressions and hand gestures. In the script, this is shown by stage directions like 'gasps' and 'holds her hands up as if in defeat'.

Make sure you mention a range of relevant features.

For scripted talk, looking at what's been left out can tell you just as much as what's been included.

It is interesting that there are none of the fillers or overlap that you would expect to find in spontaneous speech. This is probably because putting these in would make the script less clear and harder for the audience to follow.

Write a brief conclusion to sum up your findings.

As expected, the script contains lots of language features which are intended to make it sound more like spontaneous speech. These include non-fluency features, regional dialect and indications of how stress, intonation and non-verbal communication should be used. These are used carefully so that they make the dialogue sound natural and engaging without making it too long or confusing for the audience.

I have a dream today — that I'll get top marks in my GCSE...

Remember that the spoken genres questions won't just be about the scripts of TV shows. You might make a transcript of a radio advert or a public speech, for example.

Sample Task — Multi-Modal Talk

The last pair of tasks that you can choose from will both be on multi-modal talk.

Here is an Example of what you can Expect...

Investigate the language of online talk. How does it relate to spoken conversations?

1) The best data for this could be taken from your own examples of texts and online chat.

2) You'll probably want to analyse a longer extract than the one we've looked at below.

...and Here's what your Data might look like

The data from this extract was taken from an instant messenger conversation between a father and son (who is away at university).

DAD: Hi Will

WILL: hey

DAD: What u up to?

WILL: workin. Got an essay 2 b in tomoz. Then I'm finishd 4 the yr :-)

DAD: Then exams?

WILL: No exams this yr!!!

DAD: What a doddle! weren't like that in my day me laddie.

WILL: :P

DAD: Did mum tell u bout the cat? He's got cancer. in his ear.

WILL: Serious? :-O omg

DAD: Yep. Gotta have his ear taken off.

WILL: ah...poor Gavin :-(

DAD: Well...least it'll give him a few more years...anyway, going to China in August

WILL: work?

DAD: Yeh work. still, get 2 see a few places.

WILL: Brng us sumthin bck

DAD: Course! Stick of rock OK?!

WILL: lol

DAD: Gotta go. C u later xxx

WILL: Byeeeeeeeee! xxx

To give you an idea of what you could say about this data, there's a sample answer, on page 57.

For the 100th time, Mum — it does not mean 'lots of love'...

Iv ritten a top tip 4u 2 tel u not 2 procrastin8 wen ur revisin 4 ur xams. lol. also if uv bin payin @tention u shud no wot im sayin an b able 2 rite bout the dffrnt features ov my lang. :D x x x

Sample Answer — Multi-Modal Talk

Have a look at the <u>sample answer below</u>. Don't just <u>read</u> it though — <u>think</u> about what you would have said if you had <u>analysed</u> the same data and how you might have <u>structured</u> your answer too.

Remember to Focus your answer on Multi-Modal Talk

Set out your aims near the start.

Online talk is a type of multi-modal talk — it's a written form that contains elements of spoken language. I chose to look at an instant messenger conversation between my brother and my father, because I thought it might provide an interesting comparison of the amount and type of 'netspeak' used by people from different age groups. I also want to look at the similarities and differences between online conversations and spoken ones.

Talking about the overall structure of the chat before you go into the detail is a good idea.

The conversation opens with the phatic (small talk) expressions 'Hi' and 'hey', which show that the relationship between the people is informal and friendly. For the rest of the conversation the people take turns, sometimes using a question at the end of a message to show that they have finished typing, e.g. 'What u up to?'. This suggests that even though online talk is a relatively modern multi-modal form, it still follows the conventions of a traditional conversation.

Make sure you give examples to back up every point you make.

Suggesting other reasons for the patterns you've mentioned shows that you've really thought about what the data mean.

Omitting letters (e.g. 'workin', 'yr') and phonetic spelling (e.g. '2' instead of 'to' and 'c u' instead of 'see you') are used by both people, but my brother uses them more than my father. Will also uses a lot of acronyms and initialisms (e.g. 'lol', 'omg'), which are time-saving devices. This could be related to his age, but it could also be because Will is busy writing an essay, so he's more concerned with saving time than my dad is.

Both people use ellipsis (they miss out words) and simple sentences, e.g. 'get 2 see a few places' instead of 'I'll get to see a few places', and 'work?' rather than 'Is it for work?'. My brother tends to shorten sentences more than my father. In some places, this could lead to misinterpretation, for example, where he says 'Serious?' it is unclear whether he means 'Are you serious?' or 'Is it [the cancer] serious?'. This is quite common in online communication — in a spoken conversation you would be able to get the meaning across using paralinguistic features like tone of voice.

Good use of paragraphs.

Use the proper names for things wherever you can.

Will uses emoticons (e.g. :-), :-O) a lot to suggest his facial expression, whereas these don't feature in any of my father's messages. Paralinguistic features are shown using non-standard punctuation and spelling. For example, Will says 'No exams this year!!!', emphasising his excitement about this, and my father says 'Stick of rock OK?!' to show that he is joking. Will writes 'Byeeeeeeeee!' to light-heartedly suggest how he might actually pronounce the word if it was a spoken conversation. Another interesting feature of my father's netspeak is that he code-switches to non-standard English to suggest regional dialect in the sentence 'weren't like that in my day me laddie'. He seems to do this for comic effect.

Sum up what you've found out at the end.

Overall, netspeak features like clipping, non-standard punctuation and simple sentences were used by both people, but emoticons and initialisms were used only by the younger person. This suggests that netspeak is used more by younger people than by older people, just like non-standard English and slang are used more in speech by young people than by older people.

No cats were harmed in the making of this book...

Well — not as far as I know... As you might have guessed, I'm struggling to think of anything fun to say on these pages. It's all a bit serious, but don't despair — you've nearly finished the book.

Glossary

accent	The way that words are <u>pronounced</u> by a person or group. Accents can be <u>regional</u> or <u>social</u>.
address term	What people <u>call one another</u>, e.g. you might call your friend 'mate', or your teacher 'Miss'.
blend word	Words that are formed by <u>combining parts</u> of other <u>words</u> — e.g. jeans + <u>leggings</u> = <u>jeggings</u>.
code-switching	<u>Talking differently</u> (using different accents or dialects) in <u>different situations</u>.
covert prestige	Gaining status in a non-obvious way by using non-standard <u>dialect</u> or <u>accent</u>, to seem more <u>down-to-earth</u> or <u>rebellious</u>.
dialect	A <u>variety of speech</u> with specific <u>vocabulary</u> and <u>grammar</u>, and sometimes an associated <u>accent</u>. Dialects can be specific to <u>geographic regions</u>, <u>age groups</u>, and <u>social</u> and <u>professional groups</u>.
dialect-levelling	What happens when different <u>dialects merge together</u> and become <u>more similar</u>.
discourse	The <u>language routine</u> that you follow in certain <u>contexts</u>, e.g. ordering food in a restaurant might involve phrases like 'Are you ready to order?', 'What are the specials?' etc.
elision	This is when certain <u>sounds</u> are <u>slurred together</u> — e.g. '<u>don't know</u>' is pronounced '<u>dunno</u>'.
ellipsis	When words are <u>missed out</u> — e.g. 'can meet later if better' instead of '<u>I</u> can meet <u>you</u> later if <u>that's</u> better'.
Estuary English	A <u>trendy accent</u> that's emerged as features of <u>Cockney</u> and <u>RP</u> accents have <u>blended</u> together.
feedback	The things that people do to show that they're <u>listening</u> to the speaker and they <u>understand</u> or <u>agree</u> with what's being said — e.g. saying 'yes', 'mm' or 'uh huh'.
fillers	Words like 'erm' and 'um', which speakers use to fill in gaps while they're thinking about what to say next. Fillers are used to stop speakers from losing their turn in a conversation.
formality	How far speech fits in with <u>accepted conventions</u> (particularly <u>Standard English</u>) — e.g. a radio documentary is likely to contain <u>more</u> Standard English and therefore be <u>more formal</u> than a chat between friends.
idiolect	An <u>individual</u> speaker's unique <u>way of speaking</u>, influenced by their <u>age</u> and <u>regional</u> and <u>social</u> background.
initialism	Phrases that have been shortened to the <u>initial letters of the word</u>, e.g. 'OMG' for 'Oh my God'. These are different from <u>acronyms</u> because <u>each letter</u> is pronounced <u>separately</u>.
interaction	The amount of <u>input</u> from different people and how they <u>act</u> and <u>react</u> to each other, e.g. a chat between friends might involve <u>lots</u> of interaction, but a blog might involve only one person communicating (and therefore <u>little</u> interaction).
jargon	<u>Specialist words</u> that relate to a particular <u>job</u> or <u>activity</u> — e.g. biologists might talk about 'antigens'.
micropause	A pause lasting <u>less than a second</u>, that's shown in this book by '<u>(.)</u>' on a transcript.
multi-modal talk	Talk that contains features of both <u>written</u> and <u>spoken</u> language, e.g. <u>text messages</u> and <u>emails</u>.

59

Glossary

non-fluency features	Things like fal-false starts, repetition, repetition and erm fillers that all break up the flow of speech.
overt prestige	Gaining status in an obvious way by using Standard English and Received Pronunciation to seem more important, intelligent or classy.
phatic talk	'Small talk' expressions like 'hello' and 'alright, mate?' They serve a social purpose in the conversation, but their actual meaning isn't really that important.
power	The relative importance of the people involved in the talk — e.g. during a job interview the interviewer holds most of the power.
pragmatics	The implied meaning behind what a speaker says (e.g. "Well, I'll leave you to it then..." means "I'm leaving"). They tend to make conversation more polite.
paralinguistic features	How words are said — things like their tone (e.g. serious or sarcastic), stress and rhythm. Things like hand gestures and eye contact also count as paralinguistic features.
public talk	Language that's written to be spoken to others — e.g. political speeches or school assembly presentations.
Received Pronunciation	Also referred to as 'RP', 'BBC English', 'Queen's English' or 'Oxford English'. The accent that is commonly associated with Standard English. RP sounds 'posh' and is seen as a high class social accent. Using it can give the speaker overt prestige.
repertoire	The different ways that a person talks in different contexts make up their repertoire, e.g. you might speak differently to a stranger in a shop than to an old friend.
slang	The informal, often rude, words that are used most in casual conversation and multi-modal talk, e.g. 'cool', 'lairy', 'naff'. Slang words go in and out of use, so it's changing all the time.
sociolect	The dialect of a particular group of speakers (e.g. a group of friends or a group of firefighters).
solidarity	When a speaker changes the way they speak in order to fit in with the people around them.
sound representation	How the noises or pronunciation that you'd use during speech are written down (e.g. during a chat room conversation) — e.g. 'YAAAAYYY', 'woop!!!'.
Standard English	A social dialect of English, typically used in writing and formal speaking, that's associated with power, education and class. It's what many people think of as 'proper' and 'correct' English.
status	The relative superiority or inferiority of one particular accent or dialect over another — e.g. accents associated with higher social classes are seen as higher status than more working-class accents and dialects.
transcript	Spoken language that has been written down so it can be studied, showing features like pauses, fillers, repetition and false starts.
turn taking	The behaviour of speakers in a conversation when they let each other speak. People often give clues to indicate that someone else should chip in.
vague language	words or phrases that fill gaps in conversation rather than helping it make sense, e.g. 'sort of', 'like'. Also non-specific words like 'lots' or 'a few'.

Index